The Wisdom of
BERTRAND RUSSELL

A SELECTION

The Wisdom of

BERTRAND RUSSELL

A SELECTION

CITADEL PRESS
Kensington Publishing Corp.
www.kensingtonbooks.com

CITADEL PRESS books are published by

Kensington Publishing Corp.
850 Third Avenue
New York, NY 10022

All Kensington titles, imprints, and distributed lines are available at special quantity discounts for bulk purchases for sales promotions, premiums, fund-raising, educational, or institutional use. Special book excerpts or customized printings can also be created to fit specific needs. For details, write or phone the office of the Kensington special sales manager: Kensington Publishing Corp., 850 Third Avenue, New York, NY 10022, attn: Special Sales Department, phone 1-800-221-2647.

Citadel Press and the Citadel logo are trademarks of Kensington Publishing Corp.

First Citadel printing: January 2002

10 9 8 7 6 5 4 3 2 1

Printed in the United States of America

Cataloging data for this title may be obtained from the Library of Congress.

ISBN 0-8065-2328-X

The Wisdom of
BERTRAND RUSSELL

A SELECTION

A

ABELARD

Abelard's view, that (apart from Scripture) dialectic is the sole road to truth, while no empiricist can accept it, had, at the time, a valuable effect as a solvent of prejudices and an encouragement to the fearless use of the intellect. Nothing outside the Scriptures, he said, is infallible; even Apostles and Fathers may err. (HWP 437)

ANARCHISM

Anarchism, as its derivation indicates, is the theory which is opposed to every kind of forcible government. It is opposed to the State as the embodiment of the force employed in the government of the community. Such government as Anarchism can tolerate must be free government, not merely in the sense that it is that of a majority, but in the sense that it is that assented to by all. (RF 33)

ANTI-SEMITISM

Anti-Semitism is not only an abomination towards the Jews but a serious loss to the nations which, by practicing it, lose the advantages that they could derive from Jewish ability and industry. It is to be hoped—I speak as one who is not a Jew—that mankind will not continue thus to waste the by no means excessive capital of human merit. (ZPS 23)

ARISTOCRACY

... but I shrink—perhaps irrationally—from the admission that, not only here and now, but always and everywhere, what is best worth having can only be enjoyed by a cultural aristocracy. Those who take this view have the advantage of avoiding conflict with the mob, but I would rather rouse its hostility in attempting to serve it than secure its tolerance by concealing a contemptuous aloofness. From a personal point of view, aloofness may be wiser philosophically and practically, but the opposite attitude is a heritage of Christianity, and one which is essential to the survival of intelligence as a social force. (POS 474)

ARISTOTLE'S ETHICS

The views of Aristotle on ethics represent, in the main, the prevailing opinions of educated and experienced men of his day. They are not, like Plato, impregnated with mystical religion; nor do they countenance such unorthodox theories as are to be found in the *Republic* concerning property and the family. Those who neither fall below nor rise above the level of decent, well-behaved citizens will find in the *Ethics* a systematic account of the principles by which they hold that their conduct should be regulated. Those who demand anything more will be disappointed. The book appeals to the respectable middle-aged, and has been used by them, especially since the seventeenth century, to repress the ardours and enthusiasms of the young. But to a man with any depth of feeling it cannot but be repulsive. (HWP 172-3)

ART

All great art and all great science springs from the passionate desire to embody what was at first an unsubstantial phantom, a beckoning beauty luring men away from safety and ease to a glorious torment. The men in whom this passion exists must not be fettered by the shackles of a utilitarian philosophy, for to their ardour we owe all that makes man great. (EEC 312-3)

ASCETIC

The man who is enjoying a good dinner or carving a statue out of marble is not thinking of matter as his enemy, but as his opportunity. The ascetic, on the contrary—who, if he is logical, is a Manichacan—condemns all pleasures that depend on matter, and regards them as due to the material part of himself, from which he strives to be liberated. This condemnation applies not only to the pleasures commonly called sensual, but to the whole realm of art, since art is bound up with sense. Such a morality is an outcome of despair, and arises only when the primitive zest for life is extinct. (POS 463)

ATHENS

The achievements of Athens in the time of Pericles are perhaps the most astonishing thing in all history. Until that time, Athens had lagged behind many other Greek cities; neither in art nor in literature had it produced any great man (except Solon, who was primarily a lawgiver). Suddenly, under the stimulus of victory and wealth and the need of reconstruction, architects, sculptors, and dramatists, who remain unsurpassed to the present day, produced works which dominated the future down to modern times. (HWP 59)

AUGUSTINE

The theory that time is only an aspect of our thoughts is one of the most extreme forms of that subjectivism which, as we have seen, gradually increased in antiquity from the time of Protagoras and Socrates onwards. Its emotional aspect is obsession with sin, which came later than its intellectual aspects. Saint Augustine exhibits both kinds of subjectivism. Subjectivism led him to anticipate not only Kant's theory of time, but Descartes' *cogito*. In his *Soliloquia* he says: "You, who wish to know, do you know you are? I know it. Whence are you? I know not. Do you feel yourself single or multiple? I know not. Do you feel yourself moved? I know not. Do you know that you think? I do." This contains not only Descartes' *cogito*, but his reply to Gassendi's *ambulo ergo sum*. As a philosopher, therefore, Augustine deserves a high place. (HWP 354-5)

AVERROES

Averroes was concerned to improve the Arabic interpretation of Aristotle, which had been unduly influenced by Neoplatonism. He gave to Aristotle the sort of reverence that is given to the founder of a religion—much more than was given even by Avicenna. He holds that the existence of God can be proved by reason independently of revelation, a view also held by Thomas Aquinas. As regards immortality, he seems to have adhered closely to Aristotle, maintaining that the soul is not immortal, but intellect *(nous)* is. This, however, does not secure *personal* immortality, since intellect is one and the same when manifested in different persons. This view, naturally, was combated by Christian philosophers. (HWP 426)

AVICENNA

Avicenna invented a formula, which was repeated by Averroes and Albertus Magnus: "Thought brings about the generality in forms." From this it might be supposed that he did not believe in universals apart from thought. This, however, would be an unduly simple view. Genera—that is, universals—are, he says, at once before things, in things, and after things. He explains this as follows: They are *before* things in God's understanding. (God decides, for instance, to create cats. This requires that He should have the idea "cat," which is thus, in this respect anterior to particular cats.) Genera are *in* things in natural objects. (When cats have been created, felinity is in each of them.) Genera are *after* things in our thought. (When we have seen many cats, we notice their likeness to each other, and arrive at the general idea "cat".) This view is obviously intended to reconcile different theories. (HWP 425)

B

BACON

Bacon's most important book, *The Advancement of Learning,* is in many ways remarkably modern. He is commonly regarded as the originator of the saying, "Knowledge is power," and though he may have had predecessors who said the same thing, he said it with new emphasis. The whole basis of his philosophy was practical: to give mankind mastery over the forces of nature by means of scientific discoveries and inventions. He held that philosophy should be kept separate from theology, not intimately blended with it as in scholasticism. He accepted orthodox religion; he was not the man to quarrel with the government on such a matter. (HWP 542)

BELIEF

"Belief," as I wish to use the word, denotes a state of mind or body, or both, in which an animal acts with reference to something not sensibly present. When I go to the station in expectation of finding a train, my action expresses a belief. (HK 113)

I propose, therefore, to treat belief as something that can be pre-intellectual, and can be displayed in the behavior of animals. I incline to think that, on occasion, a purely bodily state may deserve to be called a "belief." For example, if you walk into your room in the dark and someone has put a chair in an unusual place, you may bump into it, because your body believed there was no chair there. But the parts played by mind and body respectively in belief are not very important to separate for our present purposes. A belief, as I understand the term, is a certain kind of state of body or mind or both. To avoid verbiage, I shall call it a state of an organism, and ignore the distinction of bodily and mental factors. (HK 144-5)

BENTHAM

Bentham did not distinguish between pleasure and happiness, and resolutely refused to assign a qualitative superiority to what are called "higher" pleasures. As he put it, "quantity of pleasure being equal, pushpin is as good as poetry." None the less, his doctrine was, in practice, almost ascetic. He held that self-approbation is the greatest of pleasures. Since men tend to value present pleasures more than pleasures in the future, the wise man will exercise prudence and self-restraint. On the whole, he and his disciples sought happiness in hard work and an almost complete indifference to all pleasures of sense. This, no doubt, was a matter of temperament, not to be explained as a deduction from the doctrine; but the result was that their morality was quite as severe as that of their orthodox opponents. (FO 92-3)

BERGSON

A great part of Bergson's philosophy is merely traditional mysticism expressed in slightly novel language. The doctrine of interpenetration, according to which different things are not really separate, but are merely so conceived by the analytic intellect, is to be found in every mystic, eastern or western, from Parmenides to Mr. Bradley. (SE 66)

C

CARDINALS

The definition of cardinals as classes of classes, and the discovery that class-symbols could be "incomplete symbols," persuaded me that cardinals as entities are unnecessary. But what had really been demonstrated was something quite independent of metaphysics, which is best stated in terms of "minimum vocabularies." I mean by a "minimum vocabulary" one in which no word can be defined in terms of the others. All definitions are theoretically superfluous, and therefore the whole of any science can be expressed by means of a minimum vocabulary for that science. (MMD 14)

CASUISTRY

As a provisional definition, we may take ethics to consist of general principles which help to determine rules of conduct. It is not the business of ethics to say how a person should act in such and such specific circumstances; that is the province of casuistry. (OP 225)

CATHOLIC PHILOSOPHY

The first great period of Catholic philosophy was dominated by Saint Augustine, and by Plato among the pagans. The second period culminates in Saint Thomas Aquinas, for whom, and for his successors, Aristotle far outweighs Plato. The dualism of *The City of God*, however, survives in full force. The church represents the City of God, and politically philosophers stand for the interests of the Church. (HWP 303)

CAUSAL LAW

A "causal law," as I shall use the term, may be defined as a general principle in virtue of which, given sufficient data about certain regions of space-time, it is possible to infer something about certain other regions of space-time. The inference may be only probable, but the probability must be considerably more than a half if the principle in question is to be considered worthy to be called a "causal law." (HK 308)

CAUSE

No doubt the reason why the old "law of causality" has so long continued to pervade the books of philosophers is simply that the idea of function is unfamiliar to most of them, and therefore they seek an unduly simplified statement. There is no question of repetitions of the "same" cause producing the "same" effect; it is not in any sameness of causes and effects that the constancy of scientific law consists, but in sameness of relations. And even "sameness of relations" is too simple a phrase; "sameness of differential equations" is the only correct phrase. It is impossible to state this accurately in non-mathematical language; the nearest approach would be as follows: "There is a constant relation between the state of the universe at any constant and the rate of change in the rate at which any part of the universe is changing at that instant, and this relation is many-one, i.e. such that the rate of change in the rate of change is determinate when the state of the universe is given." If the "law of causality" is to be something actually discoverable in the practice of science, the above proposition has a better right to the name than any "law of causality" to be found in the books of philosophers. (ML 194-5)

CENSORSHIP

When power is confined to the members of one sect, there is inevitably a severe ideological censorship. Sincere believers will be anxious to spread the true faith; others will be content with outward conformity. The former attitude kills the free exercise of intelligence; the latter promotes hypocrisy. Education and literature must be stereotyped, and designed to produce credulity rather than initiative and criticism. (P 189)

CERTAINTY, EPISTEMOLOGICAL

A proposition is certain when it has the highest degree of credibility, either intrinsically or as a result of argument. Perhaps no proposition is certain in this sense; i.e., however certain it may be in relation to a given person's knowledge, further knowledge might increase its degree of credibility. We will call this kind of certainty "epistemological." (HK 396)

CERTAINTY, LOGICAL

A propositional function is certain with respect to another when the class of terms satisfying the second is part of the class of terms satisfying the first. E.g., "x is an animal" is certain in relation to "x is a rational animal." This meaning of certainty belongs to mathematical probability. We will call this kind of certainty "logical." (HK 396)

CHRISTIANITY

One thing more was necessary to complete Western civilization as it existed before modern times, and that was the peculiar relation between government and religion which came through Christianity. Christianity was originally quite non-political, since it grew up in the Roman Empire as a consolation to those who had lost national and personal liberty; and it took over from Judaism an attitude of moral condemnation towards the rulers of the world. In the years before Constantine, Christianity developed an organization to which the Christian owed a loyalty even greater than that which he owed to the State. When Rome fell, the Church preserved in a singular synthesis what had proved most vital in the civilizations of the Jews, the Greeks, and the Romans. (IPI 187)

CHURCH, THE MEDIEVAL

In the general decay of civilization that came about during the incessant wars of the sixth and succeeding centuries, it was above all the Church that preserved whatever survived of the culture of ancient Rome. The Church performed this work very imperfectly, because fanaticism and superstition prevailed among even the greatest ecclesiastics of the time, and secular learning was thought wicked. Nevertheless, ecclesiastical institutions created a solid framework, within which, in later times, a revival of learning and civilized arts became possible. (HWP 375)

CIVILIZATION

First of all, what is civilization? Its first essential character, I should say, is *forethought*. This, indeed, is what mainly distinguishes men from brutes and adults from children. But forethought being a matter of degree, we can distinguish more or less civilized nations and epochs according to the amount of it that they display. (IPI 182)

This brings me to another element which is essential to civilization, namely, *knowledge*. Forethought based upon superstition cannot count as fully civilized, although it may bring habits of mind essential to the growth of true civilization. For instance, the Puritan habit of postponing pleasures to the next life undoubtedly facilitated the accumulation of capital required for industrialism. We may then define civilization as: *A manner of life due to the combination of knowledge and forethought.* (IPI 183-4)

CLASSICAL TRADITION

The first of these, which I shall call the classical tradition, descends in the main from Kant and Hegel; it represents the attempt to adapt to present needs the methods and results of the great constructive philosophers from Plato downwards. (KEW 4)

COMMUNISM

Communism, as it has developed in Russia, is a political religion analogous to Islam. It is, however, unavoidably influenced by Byzantine tradition; and there is a possibility that the Communist party may take the place of the Church, leaving the secular government to that degree of independence of ecclesiastical authority which it possessed before the Revolution. In this, as in other matters, Russia is divided between an Eastern and a Western mentality. In so far as Russia is Asiatic, the Communist party takes the place of the caliphate; while in so far as Russia is European, the Communist party takes the place of the Church. (ESO 17)

COMMUNISM AND DEMOCRACY

Communism is not democratic. What it calls the "dictatorship of the proletariat" is in fact the dictatorship of a small minority, who become an oligarchic governing class. All history shows that government is always conducted in the interests of the governing class, except in so far as it is influenced by fear of losing its power. This is the teaching, not only of history, but of Marx. (WNCO 133-4)

COMMUNISM AND LIBERTY

Communism restricts liberty, particularly intellectual liberty, more than any other system except Fascism. The complete unification of both economic and political power produces a terrifying engine of oppression, in which there are no loopholes for exceptions. Under such a system, progress would soon become impossible, since it is the nature of bureaucrats to object to all change except increase in their own power. (WNCO 134)

COMPETITION

Competition, formerly between individual firms, is now mainly between nations, and is therefore conducted by methods quite different from those contemplated by the classical economists. . . . Modern industrialism is a struggle between nations for two things, markets and raw materials, as well as for the sheer pleasure of dominion. (I 17)

I do not think that ordinary human beings can be happy without competition, for competition has been, ever since the origin of Man, the spur to most serious activities. We should not, therefore, attempt to abolish competition, but only to see to it that it takes forms which are not too injurious. Primitive competition was a conflict as to which should murder the other man and his wife and children; modern competition in the shape of war still takes this form. But in sport, in literary and artistic rivalry, and in constitutional polities it takes forms which do very little harm and yet offer a fairly adequate outlet for our combative instinct. What is wrong in this respect is not that such forms of competition are bad, but that they form too small a part of the lives of ordinary men and women. . . . Apart from war, modern civilization has aimed increasingly at security, but I am not at all sure that the elimination of all danger makes for happiness. (AAI 22)

COMPETITIVENESS
Competitiveness is by no means wholly an evil. When it takes the form of emulation in the service of the public, or in discovery or the production of works of art, it may become a very useful stimulus, urging men to profitable effort beyond what they would otherwise make. It is only harmful when it aims at the acquisition of goods which are limited in amount, so that what one man possesses he holds at the expense of another. When competitiveness takes this form it is necessarily attended by fear, and out of fear cruelty is almost inevitably developed. (RF 160)

CONFESSIONS
The desire to obtain a confession was the basis of the tortures of the Inquisition. In Old China, torture of suspected persons was habitual, because a humanitarian Emperor had decreed that no man should be condemned except on his own confession. For the taming of the power of the police, one essential is that a confession shall never, in any circumstances, be accepted as evidence. (P 282-3)

CONFUCIANISM

Confucianism is a political religion: Confucius, as he wandered from court to court, became concerned with the problem of government, and with the instilling of such virtues as to make good government easy. (ESO 16)

CONSCIOUSNESS

Man has developed out of the animals, and there is no serious gap between him and the amoeba. Something closely analogous to knowledge and desire, as regards its effects on behaviour, exists among animals, even where what we call "consciousness" is hard to believe in; something equally analogous exists in ourselves in cases where no trace of "consciousness" can be found. It is therefore natural to suppose that, whatever may be the correct definition of "consciousness," "consciousness" is not the essence of life or mind. (AM 40)

CONSISTENCY

No one has yet succeeded in inventing a philosophy at once credible and self-consistent. Locke aimed at credibility, and achieved it at the expense of consistency. Most of the great philosophers have done the opposite. A philosophy which is not self-consistent cannot be wholly true, but a philosophy which is self-consistent can very well be wholly false. (HWP 613)

CONTEMPLATION

A habit of finding pleasure in thought rather than in action is a safeguard against unwisdom and excessive love of power, a means of preserving serenity in misfortune and peace of mind among worries. A life confined to what is personal is likely, sooner or later, to become unbearably painful; it is only by windows into a larger and less fretful cosmos that the more tragic parts of life become endurable. (IPI 49)

CONTRADICTION, LAW OF

We must now interpret the law of contradiction. We must not say, "'This is red' and 'This is not red' cannot both be true," since we are concerned to eliminate "not." We must say, "A disbelief in the sentence 'The belief that this is red and the disbelief that this is red are both true' is always true." It seems that in this way we can replace "not" and "falsehood" by "disbelief" and "the truth of a disbelief." We then reintroduce "not" and "falsehood" by definitions: the words "This is not blue" are defined as expressing disbelief in what is expressed by the words "This is blue." In this way the need of "not" as an indefinable constituent of facts is avoided. (HK124-5)

COPERNICUS

What was important in his work was the dethronement of the earth from its geometrical pre-eminence. In the long run, this made it difficult to give to man the cosmic significance assigned to him in the Christian theology, but such consequence would not have been accepted by Copernicus, whose orthodoxy was sincere, and who protested against the view that his theory contradicted the Bible. (HWP 526-7)

COSMIC PURPOSE

There is a different and vaguer conception of Cosmic Purpose as not omnipotent but slowly working its way through a recalcitrant material. This is a more plausible conception than that of a God who, though omnipotent and loving, has deliberately produced beings so subject to suffering and cruelty as the majority of mankind. I do not pretend to know that there is no such Purpose; my knowledge of the universe is too limited. (FAR 4)

With regard to Cosmic Purpose in general, in whichever of its forms, there are two criticisms to be made. In the first place, those who believe in Cosmic Purpose always think that the world will go on evolving in the same direction as hitherto; in the second place, they hold that what has already happened is evidence of the good intentions of the universe. Both these propositions are open to question. (RAS 226)

COSMOLOGICAL ARGUMENT

The cosmological argument is, at first sight, more plausible than the ontological argument, but it is less philosophical, and derives its superior plausibility only from concealing its implications. It has a formal vice, in that it starts from finite existence as its datum, and admitting this to be contingent, it proceeds to infer an existent which is not contingent. But as the premiss is contingent, the conclusion also must be contingent. This is only to be avoided by pointing out that the argument is analytic, that it proceeds from a complex proposition to one which is logically presupposed in it, and that necessary truths may be involved in those that are contingent. But such a procedure is not properly a proof of the presupposition. (PL 175)

D

DARK AGES

Our use of the phrase the "Dark Ages" to cover the period from 600 to 1000 marks our undue concentration on Western Europe. In China, this period includes the time of the Tang dynasty, the greatest age of Chinese poetry, and in many other ways a most remarkable epoch. From India to Spain, the brilliant civilization of Islam flourished. What was lost to Christendom at this time was not lost to civilization, but quite the contrary. (HWP 399)

DEATH, ATTITUDE TOWARD

At all times, a man should feel that there are matters of importance for which he lives, and that his death, or the death of wife or child, does not put an end to all that interests him in the world. If this attitude is to be genuine and profound in adult life, it is necessary that, in adolescence, a youth should be fired with generous enthusiasms, and that he should build his life and career about them. (IPI 254)

DEDUCTION

The part played by deduction in science is greater than Bacon supposed. Often, when a hypothesis has to be tested, there is a long deductive journey from the hypothesis to some consequence that can be tested by observation. Usually the deduction is mathematical, and in this respect Bacon underestimated the importance of mathematics in scientific investigation. (HWP 545)

This is why there is real utility in the process of *deduction*, which goes from the general to the general or from the general to the particular, as well as in the process of *induction*, which goes from the particular to the particular, or from the particular to the general. (PP 123)

In deduction, we have one or more propositions called *premisses*, from which we infer a proposition called the *conclusion*. (IMP 145)

DEMOCRACY, TEACHING AND THE SURVIVAL OF

The thing, above all, that a teacher should endeavor to produce in his pupils, if democracy is to survive, is the kind of tolerance that springs from an endeavor to understand those who are different from ourselves. (UE 121)

DESIRE, CONSCIOUS

A desire is called "conscious" when it is accompanied by a true belief as to the state of affairs that will bring quiescence; otherwise it is called "unconscious." (AM 76)

DESIRE, PRIMITIVE

All primitive desire is unconscious, and in human beings beliefs as to the purposes of desires are often mistaken. These mistaken beliefs generate secondary desires, which cause various interesting complications in the psychology of human desire, without fundamentally altering the character which it shares with animal desire. (AM 76)

DESIRES AND ETHICS

All systems of ethics embody the desires of those who advocate them, but this fact is concealed in a mist of words. Our desires are, in fact, more general and less purely selfish than many moralists imagine; if it were not so, no theory of ethics would make moral improvement possible. It is, in fact not by ethical theory, but by the cultivation of large and generous desires through intelligence, happiness, and freedom from fear, that men can be brought to act more than they do at present in a manner that is consistent with the general happiness of mankind. Whatever our definition of the "Good," and whether we believe it to be subjective or objective, those who do not desire the happiness of mankind will not endeavour to further it, while those who do desire it will do what they can to bring it about. (RAS 254-5)

DESPOT, VIRTUOUS

I do not think you can ever hope to have the virtuous despot because if you do have a man who is virtuous he would soon cease to be so. (TEP 4)

DETERMINISM

We can therefore now state the hypothesis of determinism, though I am afraid the statement is rather complicated. The hypothesis is as follows: There are discoverable causal laws such that, given sufficient (but not superhuman) powers of calculation, a man who knows all that is happening within a certain sphere at a certain time can predict all that will happen at the centre of the sphere during the time that it takes light to travel from the circumference of the sphere to the centre. (RAS 157)

DICTATORSHIP

History has know many dogmatic dictatorships, and their record is not encouraging. The first historical character to found a government composed of men chosen for their adherence to a certain creed was Pythagoras, who for a time established his authority over the city of Croton, exhorting the inhabitants to study geometry and eschew beans. But, whether from hatred of geometry or from love of beans, the citizens turned against him and he had to fly. A more important example was the medieval Church, which though nominally founded upon a religion of love, endeavored to enforce its tenets by means of the Inquisition. Cromwell's rule of the Saints was in many ways similar to Lenin's system: beginning with advocacy of democracy and freedom, it ended by establishing a hated military tyranny. The French Revolution, starting from the Rights of Man, produced first Robespierre and then Napoleon, neither of whom had any very noticeable respect for human rights. In all these cases the trouble came from dogmatic belief in a panacea so splendid, that any cruelty was thought permissible in bringing about the desired end. (CTR 10)

When a Russian Communist speaks of dictatorship, he means the word literally, but when he speaks of the proletariat, he means the word in a Pickwickian sense. He means the "class-conscious" part of the proletariat, i.e., the Communist Party. He includes people by no means proletarian (such as Lenin and Tchicherin) who have the right opinions, and he excludes such wage-earners as have not the right opinions, whom he classifies as lackeys of the *bourgeoisie*. (PTB 26-7)

DISCIPLINE

The fundamental idea is simple: that the right discipline consists, not in external compulsion, but in habits of mind which lead spontaneously to desirable rather than undesirable activities. (EEC 37)

Nothing of importance is ever achieved without discipline. I feel myself sometimes not wholly in sympathy with some modern educational theorists, because I think that they underestimate the part that discipline plays. But the discipline you have in your life should be one determined by your own desires and your own needs, not put upon you by society or authority. (FAH 32-3)

DIVORCE

To sum up: Where there are no children, divorce should be obtainable at the request of either party. Where there are children, the usual ground should be mutual consent; other grounds should be insanity, grave crime, habitual drunkenness, and certain other diseases. Adultery *per se* should not be a ground. (DMC 18)

DOGMA

Systems of dogma without empirical foundation, such as those of scholastic theology, Marxism, and fascism, have the advantage of producing a great degree of social coherence among their disciples. But they have the disadvantage of involving persecution of valuable sections of the population. Spain was ruined by the expulsion of the Jews and Moors; France suffered by the emigration of Huguenots after the Revocation of the Edict of Nantes; Germany would probably have been first in the field with the atomic bomb but for Hitler's hatred of Jews. (UE 19)

see RELIGION, ELEMENTS OF

DOGMATISM, CURE FOR

A good way of ridding yourself of certain kinds of dogmatism is to become aware of opinions held in social circles different from your own. When I was young, I lived much outside my own country—in France, Germany, Italy and the United States. I found this very profitable in diminishing the intensity of insular prejudice. If you cannot travel, seek out people with whom you disagree, and read a newspaper belonging to a party that is not yours. (UE 104)

DOMAIN

The class of those terms that have a given relation to something or other is called the *domain* of that relation: thus fathers are the domain of the relation of father to child, husbands are the domain of the relation of husband to wife, wives are the domain of the relation of wife to husband, and husbands and wives together are the domain of the relation of marriage. (IMP 16)

DUNS SCOTUS

Duns Scotus held that, since there is no difference between being and essence, the "principle of individuation"—i.e., that which makes one thing not identical with another—must be form, not matter. The "principle of individuation" was one of the important problems of the scholastic philosophy. In various forms, it has remained a problem to the present day. (HWP 467)

E

ECONOMIC DEMOCRACY

As I said before, the coalescence of economic and political power is an irresistible tendency in the modern world. It may be effected in an undemocratic manner by the politicians, as has happened in Russia, Italy, and Germany. It may be effected in an undemocratic manner by the plutocrats, in the countries that are nominally democratic. For the believer in democracy, the only practicable course is to advocate its happening in a democratic way, by the transference of ultimate economic power into the hands of the democratic state. (DAE 78)

ECONOMIC POWER

Let us first consider what economic power is. In former days it consisted in ownership of land or capital, but in a developed industrial community ownership does not, as a rule, confer any appreciable share of power. Economic power belongs to large corporations, in which, by various devices, the ordinary shareholders have been deprived of all effective voice in their government, which is in the hands of a small number of too often self-perpetuating directors. (DAE 76)

My view would be that the power should be diffused and democratic, and, while it is necessary technically that certain people should have executive power, they should always be under the control of the democracy and capable of being turned out. It can only be made democratic, I think, by being put under the state. I do not see any other way of making it democratic. (TEP 4)

EDUCATION

If the object were to make pupils think, rather than to make them accept certain conclusions, education would be conducted quite differently: there would be less rapidity of instruction and more discussion, more occasions when pupils were encouraged to express themselves, more attempts to make education concern itself with matters in which the pupils felt some interest. (PSR 176-7)

The scientific educator has two things to think about: in the first place, he must produce emotions in the right proportions; and in the second place, he must attach them to the right objects. The first is probably, in the last analysis, a matter of chemistry; the second is a matter of "conditioning" in the sense of Pavlov and Watson. (SAE 89)

Education, considered as a process of forming our mental habits and our outlook on the world, is to be judged successful in proportion as its outcome approximates to this ideal; in proportion, that is to say, as it gives us a true view of our place in society, of the relation of the whole human society to its non-human environment, and of the nature of the non-human world as it is in itself apart from our desires and interests. (ML 39)

Education should have two objects: first, to give definite

knowledge—reading and writing, language and mathematics, and so on; secondly, to create those mental habits which will enable people to acquire knowledge and form sound judgments for themselves. (FT 323)

EDUCATION, LIBERAL
This is the task of a liberal education: to give a sense of the value of things other than domination, to help to create wise citizens of a free community, and through the combination of citizenship with liberty in individual creativeness to enable men to give to human life that splendor which some few have shown that it can achieve. (P 305)

EDUCATION, STATE
State education is obviously necessary, but as obviously involves dangers against which there ought to be safeguards. The evils to be feared were seen in their full magnitude in Nazi Germany and are still seen in Russia. (UE 113)

EDUCATION, UNIVERSAL COMPULSORY
There must exist in a modern community a sufficient number of men who possess the technical skill required to preserve the mechanical apparatus upon which our physical comforts depend. It is, moreover, inconvenient if any large percentage of the population is unable to read and write. For these reasons we are all in favor of universal compulsory education. (UE 115)

EDUCATOR, THE
Love of power is the chief danger of the educator, as of the politician; the man who can be trusted in education must care for his pupils on their own account, not merely as potential soldiers in an army of propagandists for a cause. (P 304)

EGO

Now if there is such a thing as the Ego, it must be a particular or a system of particulars. If the latter, it can be defined, and becomes identical with what I have called a "biography." If the former, we must know of it (if we know of it at all) either by inference or by observation. I agree with Hume that I do not know of it by observation. If it is arrived at by inference, the inference is of just that kind that I seek to invalidate by the principle of substituting constructions for inferences. The basis of this principle is that, where a suitable construction is possible, this very fact invalidates the inference, since it shows that the supposed inferred entity is not necessary for the interpretation of the propositions of the science in question. (RTC 698-9)

ELECTIONS, SOVIET

Various methods are adopted in Russia for giving the victory to Government candidates. In the first place, the voting is by show of hand, so that all who vote against the Government are marked men. In the second place, no candidate who is not a Communist can have any printing done, the printing works being all in the hands of the State. In the third place, he cannot address any meetings, because the halls all belong to the State. The whole of the press is, of course, official; no independent daily is permitted. (PTB 74-5)

EMPEDOCLES

The originality of Empedocles, outside science, consists in the doctrine of the four elements and in the use of the two principles of Love and Strife to explain change. He rejected monism, and regarded the course of nature as regulated by chance and necessity rather than by purpose. In these respects his philosophy was more scientific than those of Parmenides, Plato, and Aristotle. In other respects, it is true, he acquiesced in current superstitions; but in this he was no worse than many more recent men of science. (HWP 57-8)

EMPIRICISM

Assuming "perceptive premisses" to have been adequately defined, let us return to the definition of "empiricism." My momentary knowledge consists largely of memory, and my individual knowledge consists largely of testimony. But memory, when it is veridical, is related to a previous perceptive premiss, and testimony, when it is veridical, is related to some one else's perceptive premiss. Social empiricism takes these perceptive premisses of other times or other persons as *the* empirical premisses for what is now accepted, and thus evades the problems connected with memory and testimony. (IMT 169)

In this sense, it must be admitted, empiricism as a theory of knowledge has proved inadequate, though less so than any previous theory of knowledge. Indeed, such inadequacies as we have seemed to find in empiricism have been discovered by strict adherence to a doctrine by which empiricist philosophy has been inspired: that all human knowledge is uncertain, inexact, and partial. To this doctrine we have not found any limitation whatever. (HK 507)

I will observe, however, that empiricism, as a theory of knowledge, is self-refuting. For, however it may be formulated, it must involve *some* general proposition about the dependence of knowledge upon experience; and any such proposition, if true, must have as a consequence that itself cannot be known. While, therefore, empiricism may be true, it cannot, if true, be known to be so. This, however, is a large problem. (IMT 207)

To this extent, Hume has proved that pure empiricism is

not a sufficient basis for science. But if this one principle is admitted, everything else can proceed in accordance with the theory that all our knowledge is based on experience. It must be granted that this is a serious departure from pure empiricism, and that those who are not empiricists may ask why, if one departure is allowed, others are to be forbidden. These, however, are questions not directly raised by Hume's arguments. What these arguments prove—and I do not think the proof can be controverted—is that induction is an independent logical principle, incapable of being inferred either from experience or from other logical principles, and that without this principle science is impossible. (HWP 674)

see ALL; VERIFICATION

EMPIRICISM, MODERN ANALYTIC

Modern analytical empiricism, of which I have been giving an outline, differs from that of Locke, Berkeley, and Hume by its incorporation of mathematics and its development of a powerful logical technique. It is thus able, in regard to certain problems, to achieve definite answers, which have the quality of science rather than of philosophy. It has the advantage, as compared with the philosophies of the system-builders, of being able to tackle its problems one at a time, instead of having to invent at one stroke a block theory of the whole universe. Its methods, in this respect, resemble those of science. I have no doubt that, in so far as philosophical knowledge is possible, it is by such methods, that it must be sought. I have also no doubt that, by these methods, many ancient problems are completely soluble. (HWP 834)

EMPIRICISTS

The empiricists—who are best represented by the British philosophers, Locke, Berkeley, and Hume—maintained that all our knowledge is derived from experience. . . . (PP 114)

ENDOWMENTS

Endowments have a considerable effect in making the religious side of education more conservative than it would otherwise be. The connection of religion with private property arises through the fact that men leave their money to religious bodies, and that this secures, for centuries after their death, the propagation of the particular brand of superstition in which they believed. (ESO 202)

ERASTIANISM

Erastianism is the doctrine that the Church should be subject to the State. (HWP 363)

ETERNITY, UNDER THE ASPECT OF

Spinoza, who was one of the wisest of men and who lived consistently in accordance with his own wisdom, advised men to view passing events "under the aspect of eternity." Those who can learn to do this will find a painful present much more bearable than it would otherwise be. (IWS 17)

ETHICS

We all think electricity is entirely governed by natural laws, and yet we think it is rational to put up lightning conductors. Well, I should say that an ethic is, as it were, a lightning conductor for human passions, to enable them within a deterministic world to work in a way that produces a minimum of disaster. (SPE 107)

Ethics is in origin the art of recommending to others the sacrifices required for co-operation with oneself. Hence, by reflexion, it comes, through the operation of social justice, to recommend sacrifices by oneself, but all ethics, however refined, remains more or less subjective. Even vegetarians do not hesitate, for example, to save the life of a man in a fever, although in doing so they destroy the lives of many millions of microbes. (ML 108-9)

ETHICS, CHRISTIAN

The fundamental defect of Christian ethics consists in the fact that it labels certain classes of acts "sins" and others "virtues" on grounds that have nothing to do with their social consequences. An ethic not derived from superstition must decide first upon the kind of social effects which it desires to achieve and the kind which it desires to avoid. It must then decide, as far as our knowledge permits, what acts will promote the desired consequences; these acts it will praise, while those having a contrary tendency it will condemn. (ESO 110-1)

ETHICS, MUNDANE BASIS OF

We have seen a great system of cruel falsehood, the Nazi system, lead a nation to disaster at immense cost to its opponents. It is not by such systems that happiness is to be achieved; even without the help of revelation it is not difficult to see that human welfare requires a less ferocious ethic. More and more people are becoming unable to accept traditional beliefs. If they think that, apart from these beliefs, there is no reason for kindly behaviour the results may be needlessly unfortunate. That is why it is important to show that no supernatural reasons are needed to make men kind and to prove that only through kindness can the human race achieve happiness. (FAR 6)

ETHICS, PERSONAL

I come now to the question of personal ethics, as opposed to the question of social and political institutions. No man is wholly free, and no man is wholly a slave. To the extent to which a man has freedom, he needs a personal morality to guide his conduct. There are some who would say that a man need only obey the accepted moral code of his community. But I do not think any student of anthropology could be content with this answer. Such practices as cannibalism, human sacrifice, and head hunting have died out as a result of moral protests against conventional moral opinion. If a man seriously desires to live the best life that is open to him, he must learn to be critical of the tribal customs and tribal beliefs that are generally accepted among his neighbours. (AAI 109)

ETHICS, SCIENCE AND

Science can, if rulers so desire, create sentiments which will avert disaster and facilitate cooperation. At present there are powerful rulers who have no such wish. But the possibility exists, and science can be just as potent for good as for evil. It is not science, however, which will determine how science is used. Science, by itself, cannot supply us with an ethic. It can show us how to achieve a given end, and it may show us that some ends cannot be achieved. But among ends that can be achieved our choice must be decided by other than purely scientific considerations. (STS 33)

ETHICS, SPINOZA'S

The basis of his ethic, so far as I accept his ethic is that one can discover by experience that there is a certain kind of way of living which seems to most of those who have tried it to be a good way and which is the way which

Spinoza recommends—a way in which you get rid of indignation and fear and irrational hope and a number of the things that produce anxiety and perturbation in life, and acquire a certain kind of calm. The kind of calm which Spinoza recommends is, I think, attainable without adopting his metaphysic. (SPE 112-3)

EUCLID
Euclid, who was still, when I was young, the sole acknowledged text-book of geometry for boys, lived in Alexandria, about 300 B.C., a few years after the death of Alexander and Aristotle. Most of his *Elements* was not original, but the order of propositions, and the logical structure, were largely his. The more one studies geometry, the more admirable these are seen to be. (HWP 211)

EUGENICS
Eugenics is of two sorts, positive and negative. The former is concerned with the encouragement of good stocks, the latter with the discouragement of bad ones. The latter is at present more practicable. (MM 258)

Unfortunately the concern of biology is with the most intimate part of human life, where emotions, morals, and religion alike stand in the way of progress. It may be doubted whether human nature could bear so great an interference with the life of instinct as would be involved in a really effective application of eugenics. Whatever may be thought disagreeable in the machine age would be greatly intensified by the application of science to parenthood, and men might well think the price not worth paying. (S 81)

EVENTS
We shall find, if I am not mistaken, that the objects which are mathematically primitive in physics, such as electrons,

protons, and points in space-time, are all logically complex structures composed of entities which are metaphysically more primitive, which may be conveniently called "events." (AOM 9)

And what we can primarily infer from percepts, assuming the validity of physics, are groups of events, again not substances. It is a mere linguistic convenience to regard a group of events as states of a "thing," or "substance," or "piece of matter." This inference was originally made on the ground of the logic which philosophers inherited from common sense. By defining a "thing" as the group of what would formerly have been its "states," we alter nothing in the detail of physics, and avoid an inference as precarious as it is useless. (AOM 284)

EVIL

When it is realized that the fundamental evils are due to the blind empire of matter, and are the wholly necessary effects of forces which have no consciousness and are therefore neither good nor bad in themselves, indignation becomes absurd, like Xerxes chastising the Hellespont. Thus the realisation of necessity is the liberation from indignation. This alone, however, will not prevent an undue preoccupation with evil. It is obvious that some things that exist are good, some bad, and we have no means of knowing whether the good or the bad preponderate. (ER 57)

F

FACT

I mean by a "fact" something which is there, whether anybody thinks so or not. If I look up a railway timetable and find that there is a train to Edinburgh at 10 A.M., then, if the timetable is correct, there is an actual train, which is a "fact." The statement in the timetable is itself a "fact," whether true or false, but it only *states* a fact if it is true, i.e., if there really is a train. Most facts are independent of our volitions; that is why they are called "hard," "stubborn," or "ineluctable." Physical facts, for the most part, are independent, not only of our volitions but even of our existence. (HK 143)

FACTUAL PREMISS

I shall give the name "factual premise" to any uninferred proposition which asserts something having a date and which I believe after a critical scrutiny. I do not mean that the date is part of the assertion, but merely that some kind of temporal occurrence is what is involved in the truth of the assertion. (IMT 190)

FALSEHOOD

The ultimate test of falsehood is *never,* I think, the nature of the consequences of a belief, but the association between words and sensible or remembered facts. A belief is "verified" when a situation arises which gives a feeling of expectedness in connection with it; it is falsified when the feeling is one of surprise. But this only applies to beliefs which await some future contingency for verification or refutation. (OP 258)

FAMILY RELATION

A man and woman who love each other and their children ought to be able to act spontaneously as the heart dictates. They will need much thought and knowledge, but these they will acquire out of parental affection. They must not demand from their children what they get from each other, but if they are happy in each other they will feel no impulse to do so. If the children are properly cared for, they will feel for their parents a natural affection which will be no barriers to independence. What is needed is not ascetic self-denial, but freedom and expansiveness of instinct, adequately informed by intelligence and knowledge. (EEC 198)

FASCISM

Fascism is a complex movement; its German and Italian forms differ widely, and in other countries, if it spreads, it may assume still other shapes. It has, however, certain essentials, without which it would cease to be Fascism. It is anti-democratic, it is nationalistic, it is capitalistic, and it appeals to those sections of the middle class which suffer through modern developments and expect to suffer still more if Socialism or Communism become established. Communism, also, is anti-democratic, but only for a time, at least, so far as its theoretical statements can be accepted as giving its real policy; moreover, it aims at serving the interests of wage-earners, who are a majority in advanced countries, and are intended by Communists to become the whole population. Fascism is anti-democratic in a more fundamental sense. It does not accept the greatest happiness of the greatest number as the right principle in statesmanship, but selects certain individuals, nations, and classes as "the best," and as alone worthy of consideration. The remainder are to be compelled by force to serve the interests of the elect. (IPI 130-1)

FASCISM, ANCESTORS OF

The founders of the school of thought out of which Fascism has grown all have certain common characteristics. They seek the good in *will* rather than in feeling or cognition; they value power more than happiness; they prefer force to argument, war to peace, aristocracy to democracy, propaganda to scientific impartiality. They advocate a Spartan form of austerity, as opposed to the Christian form; that is to say, they view austerity as a means of obtaining mastery over others not as a self-discipline which helps to produce virtue, and happiness only in the next world. The later ones among them are imbued with popular Darwinism, and regard the struggle for existence as the source of a higher species; but it is to be rather a struggle between races than one between individuals, such as the apostles of free competition advocated. Pleasure and knowledge, conceived as ends, appear to them unduly passive. For pleasure they substitute glory, and, for knowledge, the pragmatic assertion that what they desire is true. In Fichte, Carlyle, and Mazzini, these doctrines are still enveloped in a mantle of conventional moralistic cant; in Nietzsche they first step forth naked and unashamed. (IPI 104-5)

FATE

The notion of fate or destiny is one which has hung over mankind from ancient times. The Greeks thought of it as superior even to the gods and holding sway over Zeus as well as over mortals. It was reinforced when, after Alexander's conquests in the East, astrology became fashionable. It came to be thought that the stars control human affairs and that a man born under such and such a star was bound to have a life in conformity with his horoscope . . . This conception, very rightly, was vigorously opposed by the Church, since it seemed to relieve a man of moral responsibility. (TRF 5)

FEAR AND RELIGION

Religion is based, I think, primarily and mainly upon fear. It is partly the terror of the unknown, and partly, as I have said, the wish to feel that you have a kind of elder brother who will stand by you in all your troubles and disputes. Fear is the basis of the whole thing—fear of the mysterious, fear of defeat, fear of death. Fear is the parent of cruelty, and therefore it is no wonder if cruelty and religion go hand-in-hand. (WNC 29)

FEAR, DISASTROUS RESULTS OF

Intellectually, also, fear has disastrous results. There is the fear of any unusual opinion which prevents men from thinking straight on any subject on which their neighbors have foolish opinions. Then there is the fear of death, which prevents men from thinking straight on theological subjects; and then there is the fear of self-direction, which leads men to seek some authority to which they can submit their judgment. These various forms of fear are responsible for quite half the stupidity in the world. (EDTF 229-30)

FEAR, EFFECT OF

There are various kinds of fear; of these, physical fear, which alone is traditionally despised, is by far the least harmful. Moral and intellectual fears are far worse. All fear inspires a greater or less degree of rage, which, since it dare not vent itself upon the dreaded object, finds an outlet in tyranny over whatever is weaker. Just as in the holders of power cruelty begets fear, so in their slaves fear begets cruelty. Fear of social disapproval is probably one of the chief causes of meanness and unkindness in the modern world. (EDTF 220-1)

FEDERALISM

The problem of delimiting the powers of various bodies will, of course, be one presenting many difficulties. The general principle should be to leave to smaller bodies all functions which do not prevent the larger bodies from fulfilling their purpose. Confining ourselves, for the moment, to geographical bodies, there should be a hierarchy from the world government to parish councils. (AAI 99)

In international affairs the same formula of federalism will apply: self-determination for every group in regard to matters which concern it much more vitally than they concern others, and government by a neutral authority embracing rival groups in all matters in which conflicting interest of groups come into play; but always with the fixed principle that the functions of government are to be reduced to the bare minimum compatible with justice and the prevention of private violence. (RF 161)

A federal system is desirable whenever the local interests and sentiments of the constituent units are stronger than the interests and sentiments connected with the federation. If there were ever an international government, it would obviously have to be a federation of national governments, with strictly defined powers. (P 280)

FEELING OF KNOWLEDGE AND OF DOUBT

Whether a sentence gives us a *feeling* of knowledge or of doubt depends upon whether it leaves open alternatives calling for different actions and emotions or not. Every disjunction which is not logically exhaustive (i.e., not such as "A or not-A") gives *some* information about the world, if it is true, but the information may leave us so hesitant as to what to do that it is *felt* as ignorance. (IMT 106)

FREE WILL

The first dogma which I came to disbelieve was that of free will. It seemed to me that all motions of matter were determined by the laws of dynamics and could not therefore be influenced by the human will, even in the instance of matter forming part of a human body. I had never heard of Cartesianism, or, indeed, of any of the great philosophies, but my thoughts ran spontaneously on Cartesian lines. (WIBII 10)

FREEDOM

From the submission of our desires springs the virtue of resignation; from the freedom of our thoughts springs the whole world of art and philosophy, and the vision of beauty by which, at last, we half reconquer the reluctant world. But the vision of beauty is possible only to unfettered contemplation, to thoughts not weighted by the load of eager wishes; and thus Freedom comes only to those who no longer ask life that it shall yield them any of those personal goods that are subject to the mutations of Time. (ML 51)

FREEDOM, MENTAL

In everything that lies outside the provision of the necessaries of life, there must be individualism, personal initiative, variety. The fight for freedom is not to be won by any mere change in our economic system. It is to be won only by a constant resistance to the tyranny of officials, and a constant realization that mental freedom is the most precious of all goods. (FIE 163-4)

FREEDOM OF OPINION

Freedom of opinion is closely connected with free speech, but has a wider scope. The Inquisition made a point of investigating, by means of torture, the secret opinions that men endeavored to keep to themselves. When men confessed to unorthodox opinions, they were punished even if it could not be proved that they had ever before given utterance to them. This practice has been revived in the dictatorial countries, Germany, Italy, and Russia. The reason, in each case, is that the government feels itself unstable. One of the most important conditions of freedom, in the matter of opinion as in other matters, is governmental security. (FAG 255)

FUNCTION, NEGATIVE

The simplest of such functions is the negative, "not-p." This is that function of p which is true when p is false, and false when p is true. (IMP 146)

FUNCTION, PROPOSITIONAL

A "propositional function," in fact, is an expression containing one or more undetermined constituents, such that, when values are assigned to these constituents, the expression becomes a proposition. In other words, it is a function whose values are propositions. (IMP 155-6)

FUNCTIONS, DESCRIPTIVE AND PROPOSITIONAL

The notion of *function* need not be confined to numbers, or to the uses to which mathematicians have accustomed us; it can be extended to all cases of one-many relations.

G

GALILEO

Galileo was the first to establish the law of falling bodies. This law, given the concept of "acceleration," is of the utmost simplicity. It says that, when a body is falling freely, its acceleration is constant, except in so far as the resistance of the air may interfere; further, the acceleration is the same for all bodies, heavy or light, great or small. The complete proof of this law was not possible until the air pump had been invented, which was about 1654. After this, it was possible to observe bodies falling in what was practically a vacuum, and it was found that feathers fall as fast as lead. (HWP 532)

GOD

If everything must have a cause, then God must have a cause. If there can be anything without a cause, it may just as well be the world as God, so that there cannot be any validity in that argument. It is exactly of the same nature as the Indian's view, that the world rested upon an elephant and the elephant rested upon a tortoise; and when they said, "How about the tortoise?" the Indian said, "Suppose we change the subject." The argument is really no better than that. (WNC 11)

There are, roughly speaking, two functions which a Christian God has to fulfil. He has to be a Providence and a Creator. Leibniz merged the first of these functions in the second, though he often denied that he had done so. (PL 183)

Why did God issue just those natural laws and no others? If you say that he did it simply from his own good pleasure, and without any reason, you then find that there is something which is not subject to law, and so your train of natural law is interrupted. If you say, as more orthodox theologians do, that in all the laws which God issued he had a reason for giving those laws rather than others—the reason, of course, being to create the best universe, although you would never think it to look at it—if there was a reason for the laws which God gave, then God himself was subject to law, and therefore you do not get any advantage by introducing God as intermediary. (WNC 13-4)

When you come to look into this argument from design, it is a most astonishing thing that people can believe that this world, with all the things that are in it, with all its defects, should be the best that omnipotence and omniscience has been able to produce in millions of years. I really cannot believe it. (WNC 15)

GOOD, DOING

Our motives in doing good are seldom as pure as we imagine them to be. Love of power is insidious; it has many disguises, and is often the source of the pleasure we derive from doing what we believe to be good to other people. Not infrequently, yet another element enters in. "Doing good" to people generally consists in depriving them of some pleasure: drink, or gambling, or idleness, or what not. In this case there is an element which is typical of much social morality, namely, envy of those who are in a position to commit sins from which we have to abstain if we are to retain the respect of our friends. (CH 117)

GOOD LIFE, THE

To live a good life in the fullest sense a man must have a good education, friends, love, children (if he desires them), a sufficient income to keep him from want and grave anxiety, good health, and work which is not uninteresting. All these things, in varying degrees, depend upon the community, and are helped or hindered by political events. The good life must be lived in a good society and is not fully possible otherwise. (WIB 60-1)

The good life is one inspired by love and guided by knowledge. (WIB 20)

GOVERNMENT, THE PRIMARY AIMS OF

The *primary* aims of government, I suggest, should be three: security, justice, and conservation.

GREAT MEN

The great are not solitary; out of the night come the voices of those who have gone before, clear and courageous; and so through the ages they march, a mighty procession, proud, undaunted, unconquerable. To join in this glorious company, to swell the immortal paeon of those whom fate could not subdue—this may not be happiness; but what is happiness to those whose souls are filled with that celestial music? (OH 213-4)

GREEK CIVILIZATION

The distinctive Western character begins with the Greeks, who invented the habit of deductive reasoning and the science of geometry. Their other merits were either not distinctive or lost in the Dark Ages. In literature and art they may have been supreme, but they did not differ very profoundly from various other ancient nations. In experimental science they produced a few men, notably Archimedes, who anticipated modern methods, but these men did not succeed in establishing a school or a tradition. (IPI 185-6)

H

HABIT
All kinds of matter to some extent, but some kinds of matter (viz. nervous tissue) more particularly, are liable to form "habits," i.e. to alter their structure in a given environment in such a way that, when they are subsequently in a similar environment, they react in a new way, but if similar environments recur often, the reaction in the end becomes nearly uniform, while remaining different from the reaction on the first occasion. (LA 381)

HABIT FORMATION IN INFANCY
Two considerations come in when we are considering habit-formation in infancy. The first and paramount consideration is health; the second is character. We want the child to become the sort of person that will be liked and will be able to cope with life successfully. Fortunately, health and character point in the same direction: what is good for one is good also for the other. (EEC 89-90)

HABITS, ACQUIRED

Our habitual knowledge is not always in our minds, but is called up by the appropriate stimuli. If we are asked "What is the capital of France?" we answer "Paris," because of past experience; the past experience is as essential as the present question in the causation of our response. Thus all our habitual knowledge consists of acquired habits, and comes under the head of mnemic phenomena. (AM 79-80)

HAPPINESS

Happiness, if it is to have any depth and solidity, demands a life built round some central purpose of a kind demanding continuous activity and permitting of progressively increasing success. The purpose must be one which has its root in instinct, such as love of power or love of honour, or parental affection. (WIH 59)

Fundamental happiness depends more than anything else upon what may be called a friendly interest in persons and things. (CH 155)

The secret of happiness is this: let your interests be as wide as possible, and let your reactions to the things and persons that interest you be as far as possible friendly rather than hostile. (CH 157)

HARMONY IN LIFE

If a man's life is to be satisfactory, whether from his own point of view or from that of the world at large, it requires two kinds of harmony: an internal harmony of intelligence, emotion, and will, and an external harmony with the wills of others. In both these respects, existing education is defective. (ESO 237)

HATRED, PSYCHOLOGY OF

We must therefore find some other non-human object of hatred, if men are to be prevented from hating their neighbours in other countries. One might hate matter, like the Manicheans, or ignorance, or disease. To hate these things would do good; and by a little symbolism it could be made to satisfy our instinctive craving for hatred. But to hate other groups of human beings can only do harm, and it is monstrous that education should aim at instilling suck hatred by means of lies and suppressions. (FIE 157)

HEGEL

Hegel asserts that the real is rational, and the rational is real. But when he says this he does not mean by "the real" what an empiricist would mean. He admits, and even urges, that what to the empiricist appear to be facts are, and must be, irrational; it is only after their apparent character has been transformed by viewing them as aspects of the whole that they are seen to be rational. Nevertheless, the identification of the real and the rational leads unavoidably to some of the complacency inseparable from the belief that "whatever is, is right." (HWP 731)

HERACLITUS

Heraclitus himself, for all his belief in change, allowed *something* everlasting. The conception of eternity (as opposed to endless duration), which comes from Parmenides, is not to be found in Heraclitus, but in his philosophy the central fire never dies: the world "was ever, is now, and ever shall be, an ever-living Fire." But fire is something continually changing, and its permanence is rather that of a process than that of a substance—though this view should not be attributed to Heraclitus. (HWP 46)

HERE

It is to be observed that "here" and "now" depend upon perception; in a purely material universe there would be no "here" and "now." Perception is not impartial, but proceeds from a center; our perceptual world is (so to speak) a perspective view of the common world. (HK 92)

We may define "here" as the place, in perspective space, which is occupied by our private world. Thus we can now understand what is meant by speaking of a thing as near to or far from "here." (KEW 97)

HEREDITARY

A property is said to be "hereditary" in the natural-number series if, whenever it belongs to a number n, it also belongs to $n + 1$, the successor of n. Similarly a class is said to be "hereditary" if, whenever n is a member of the class, so is $n + 1$. (IMP 21)

HISTORY

History has always interested me more than anything else except philosophy and mathematics. I have never been able to accept any general scheme of historical development, such as that of Hegel or that of Marx. Nevertheless, general trends can be studied, and the study is profitable in relation to the present. (MMD 18-9)

I have seen cruelty, persecution, and superstition increasing by leaps and bounds, until we have almost reached the point where praise of rationality is held to mark a man as an old fogey regrettably surviving from a bygone age. All this is depressing, but gloom is a useless emotion. In order to escape from it, I have been driven to study the past with more attention than I had formerly given to it, and have found, as Erasmus found, that folly is perennial and yet the human race has survived. That follies of our times are easier to bear when they are seen against the background of past follies. (UE 71)

HOBBES

Hobbes prefers monarchy, but all his abstract arguments are equally applicable to all forms of government in which there is one supreme authority not limited by the legal rights of other bodies. He could tolerate Parliament alone, but not a system in which governmental power is shared between king and Parliament. This is the exact antithesis to the views of Locke and Montesquieu. The English Civil War occurred, says Hobbes, because power was divided between King, Lord, and Commons. (HWP 551)

HOLMES, OLIVER WENDELL

I will only say, to begin with, that Europeans with pretensions to culture are too apt to remember Hollywood with a sniff, and forget the respect due to such men as Holmes, who was, after all, equally a product of America. (PCI 3)

HOMER

The first notable product of the Hellenic civilization was Homer. Everything about Homer is conjectural, but the best opinion seems to be that he was a series of poets rather than an individual. Probably the Iliad and the Odyssey between them took about two hundred years to complete, some say from 750 to 550 B. C., while others hold that "Homer" was nearly complete at the end of the eighth century. (HWP 10)

HONESTY

A rather more serious matter, to which similar considerations apply, is honesty. I do not mean this term in any fancy sense; I mean merely respect for the property of others. This is not a natural characteristic of human beings. The undisciplined human being appropriates the property of others whenever he considers it safe to do so. Perhaps even the disciplined human being does this not infrequently, but discipline has taught him that theft is often not safe when at first sight it seems so. (ESO 36)

HOPE

And so, to the man tempted by despair, I say: Remind yourself that the world is what we make it, and that to the making of it each one of us can contribute something. This thought makes hope possible: and in this hope, though life will still be painful, it will be no longer purposeless. (APFY 7)

HUMAN EXCELLENCE

At the same time, when I examine my own conception of human excellence, I find that, doubtless owing to early environment, it contains many elements which have hitherto been associated with aristocracy, such as fearlessness, independence of judgment, emancipation from the herd, and leisurely culture. Is it possible to preserve these qualities, and even make them widespread, in an industrial community? And is it possible to dissociate them from the typical aristocratic vices: limitation of sympathy, haughtiness, and cruelty to those outside a charmed circle? These bad qualities could not exist in a community in which the aristocratic virtues were universal. But that could only be achieved through economic security and leisure, which are the two sources of what is good in aristocracies. It has at last become technically possible through the progress of machinery and the consequent increased productivity of labor, to create a society in which every man and woman has economic security and sufficient leisure—for complete leisure is neither necessary nor desirable. But although the technical possibility exists, there are formidable political and psychological obstacles. It would be necessary to the creation of such a society to secure three conditions: first, a more even distribution of the produce of labor; second, security against large-scale wars; and third, a population which is stationary or very nearly so. (ISP xv-xvi)

HUMAN NATURE, TRANSFORMATION OF

The ultimate source of the whole train of evils lies in the Bolshevik outlook on life: in its dogmatism of hatred and its belief that human nature can be completely transformed by force. (PTB 180)

If human nature were unchangeable, as ignorant people still suppose it to be, the situation would indeed be hopeless. But we now know, thanks to psychologists and physiologists, that what passes as "human nature" is at most one-tenth nature, the other nine-tenths being nurture. What is called human nature can be almost completely changed by changes in early education. And these changes could be such as to preserve sufficient seriousness in life without the spice of danger, if thought and energy were devoted to that end. Two things are necessary for this purpose: the development of constructive impulses in the young, and opportunities for their existence in adult life. (SE 254-5)

HUMAN RACE, THE

Unfortunately, there is no impartial arbiter to decide on the merits of the human race; but for my part, when I consider their poison gases, their researches into bacteriological warfare, their meanness, cruelties and oppressions, I find them, considered as the crowning gem of creation, somewhat lacking in lustre. (SO 122)

HUMANISM

Those who attempt to make a religion of humanism, which recognizes nothing greater than man, do not satisfy my emotions. And yet I am unable to believe that, in the world as known, there is anything that I can value outside human beings, and, to a much lesser extent, animals. Not the starry heavens, but their effects on human percipients, have excellence; to admire the universe for its size is slavish and absurd; impersonal non-human truth appears to be a delusion. And so my intellect goes with the humanists, though my emotions violently rebel. In this respect the "consolations of philosophy" are not for me. (MMD 19-20)

I

I

... "I" is the biography to which "this" belongs. But although we have explained the use of the word "this," we have done so by depriving the word itself of all significance in isolation. We cannot therefore be sure that the above definition of "I" can be maintained. (IMT 141)

IDEA

He (Berkeley) gives the name "idea" to anything which is *immediately* known, as, for example, sense-data are known. (PP 61)

IDEA, GENERAL

Thus we may say that a word embodies a vague idea when its effects are appropriate to an individual, but are the same for various similar individuals, while a word embodies a general idea when its effects are different from those appropriate to individuals. In what this difference consists it is, however, not easy to say. I am inclined to think that it consists merely in the knowledge that no one individual is represented, so that what distinguishes a general idea from a vague idea is merely the presence of a certain accompanying belief. (AM 221-2)

IDEAL, RUSSIAN

The Russian Government has a different conception of the ends of life. The individual is thought of no importance; he is expendable. What is important is the state, which is regarded as something almost divine and having a welfare of its own not consisting in the welfare of citizens. This view, which Marx took over from Hegel, is fundamentally opposed to the Christian ethic, which in the West is accepted by free thinkers as much as by Christians. In the Soviet world human dignity counts for nothing. (IWS 17)

IDEAL, WESTERN

In the West, we see man's greatness in the individual life. A great society for us is one which is composed of individuals who, as far as is humanly possible, are happy, free and creative. We do not think that individuals should be alike. We conceive society as like an orchestra, in which the different performers have different parts to play and different instruments upon which to perform, and in which cooperation results from a conscious common purpose. (IWS 5)

IDEALISM

We can begin to state the difference between realism and idealism in terms of this opposition of contents and objects. Speaking quite roughly and approximately, we may say that idealism tends to suppress the object, while realism tends to suppress the content. Idealism, accordingly, says that nothing can be known except thoughts, and all the reality that we know is mental; while realism maintains that we know objects directly, in sensation certainly, and perhaps in memory and thought. (AM 19-20)

IDEAS

From memory it is an easy step to what are called "ideas"—not in the Platonic sense, but in that of Locke, Berkeley and Hume, in which they are opposed to "impressions." You may be conscious of a friend either by seeing him or by "thinking" of him; and by "thought" you can be conscious of objects which cannot be seen, such as the human race, or physiology. "Thought" in the narrower sense is that form of consciousness which consists in "ideas" as opposed to impressions or mere memories. (AM 13)

IMAGES

Images, as opposed to sensations, can only be defined by their different causation: they are caused by association with a sensation, not by a stimulus external to the nervous system—or perhaps one should say external to the brain, where the higher animals are concerned. The occurrence of a sensation or image does not in itself constitute knowledge but any sensation or image may come to be known if the conditions are suitable. (AM 109-10)

Images come in various ways, and play various parts. There are those that come as accretions to a case of sensation, which are not recognised as images except by the psychologist; these form, for example, the factual quality of things we only see, and the visual quality of things we only touch. I think dreams belong, in part, to this class of images: some dreams result from misinterpreting some ordinary stimulus, and in these cases the images are those suggested by a sensation, but suggested more uncritically than if we were awake. Then there are images which are not attached to a present reality, but to one which we locate in the past; these are present in memory, not necessarily always, but sometimes. Then there are images not attached to reality at all so far as our feeling about them goes: images which merely float into our heads in reverie or in passionate desire. And finally there are images which are called up voluntarily, for example, in considering how to decorate a room. (OP 186)

IMMORTALITY

What science has to say on the subject of immortality is not very definite. There is, indeed, one line of argument in favour of survival after death, which is, at least in intention, completely scientific—I mean the line of argument associated with psychical research. I have not myself sufficient knowledge on this subject to judge of the evidence already available, but it is clear that there could be evidence which would convince reasonable men. To this, however, certain provisos must be added. In the first place, the evidence, at the best, would prove only that we survive death, not that we survive forever. (RAS 141-2)

Believers in immortality will object to physiological arguments, such as I have been using, on the ground that soul and body are totally disparate, and that the soul is something quite other than its empirical manifestations through our bodily organs. I believe this to be a metaphysical superstition. Mind and matter alike are for certain purposes convenient terms, but are not ultimate realities. Electrons and protons, like the soul, are logical fictions; each is really a history, a series of events, not a single persistent entity. (WIB 9)

Immortality, if we could believe in it, would enable us to shake off this gloom about the physical world. We should hold that although our souls, during their sojourn here on earth are in bondage to matter and physical laws, they pass from earth into an eternal world beyond the empire of decay which science seems to reveal in the sensible world.

But it is impossible to believe this unless we think that a human being consists of two parts—soul and body—which are separable and can continue independently of each other. Unfortunately all the evidence is against this. (FAR 5)

If there is a future life, and if heaven is the reward for misery here below, we do right to obstruct all amelioration of terrestrial conditions, and we must admire the unselfishness of those captains of industry who allow others to monopolise the profitable brief sorrow on earth. But if the belief in a hereafter is mistaken, we shall have thrown away the substance for the shadow, and shall be as unfortunate as those who invest a life-time's savings in enterprises that go bankrupt. (ESO 108-9)

IMPERIALISM

The imperialism of single nations, such as the British, the French, and the Dutch, has become an anachronism, and an invitation to war, because it is no longer backed by irresistible military force. But in certain parts of the world, if there is not to be dangerous chaos, national imperialism will have to be succeeded by an international control. The principle of national independence, if treated as absolute, is anarchic, and makes the prevention of war impossible. (ISIP 232)

IMPLICATION

Last take *implication,* i.e., "p implies q" or "if p, then q." This is to be understood in the widest sense that will allow us to infer the truth of q if we know the truth of p. Thus we interpret it as meaning: "Unless p is false, q is true," or "either p is false or q is true." (The fact that "implies" is capable of other meanings does not concern us; this is the meaning which is convenient for us.) That is to say, "p implies q" is to mean "not-p or q": its truth-value is to be truth if p is false, likewise if q is true, and is to be falsehood if p is true and q is false. (IMP 147)

IMPULSES

There are two kinds of impulses, corresponding to the two kinds of goods. There are *possessive* impulses, which aim at acquiring or retaining private goods that cannot be shared; these center in the impulse of property. And there are *creative* or constructive impulses, which aim at bringing into the world or making available for use the kind of goods in which there is no privacy and no possession. (PI 8)

IMPULSES, REPRESSIVE

I think that if we are going to have a true morality, if we are going to have an outlook upon life which is going to make life richer and freer and happier, it must not be a repressive outlook, it must not be an outlook based upon any kind of restrictions or prohibitions; it must be an outlook based upon the things that we love rather than those that we hate. There are a number of emotions which guide our lives, and roughly you can divide them into those that are repressive and those that are expansive. Repressive emotions are cruelty, fear, jealousy; expansive emotions are such as hope, love of art, impulse of constructiveness, love, affection, intellectual curiosity, and kindliness; and they make more of life instead of less. I think that the essence of true morality consists in living by the expansive impulses and not by the repressive ones. (FAH 23-4)

INCARNATION, DOCTRINE OF THE

At last Pope Leo—the same Pope who turned Attila from attacking Rome—in the year of the battle of Chalons secured the summoning of an oecumenical Council at Chalcedon in 451, which condemned the Monophysites and finally decided the orthodox doctrine of the Incarnation. The Council of Ephesus had decided that there is only one *Person* of Christ, but the Council of Chalcedon decided that He exists in two *natures*, one human and one divine. The influence of the Pope was paramount in securing this decision. (HWP 369)

INCOMPATIBILITY

Take next *incompatibility*, i.e. "p and q are not both true." This is negation of conjunction; it is also the disjunction of the negations of p and q, i.e. it is "not-p or not-q." Its truth-value is truth when p is false and likewise when q is false; its truth-value is falsehood when p and q are both true. (IMP 147)

INDETERMINACY, PRINCIPLE OF

The Principle of Indeterminacy states that it is impossible to determine with precision both the position and the momentum of a particle; there will be a margin of error in each, and the product of the two errors is constant. That is to say, the more accurately we determine the one, the less accurately we shall be determining the other, and *vice versa*. The margin of error involved is, of course, very small. (SO 104)

INDIVIDUALISM, LOSS OF

There is one regrettable feature of scientific civilization as hitherto developed: I mean, the diminution in the value and independence of the individual. Great enterprises tend more and more to be collective, and in an industrialized world the interference of the community with the individual must be more intense than it need be in a commercial or agricultural regime. Although machinery makes man collectively more lordly in his attitude towards nature, it tends to make the individual man more submissive to his group. (S 77-8)

INDIVIDUATION

Among the properties of individual things, some are essential, others accidental; the accidental properties of a thing are those it can lose without losing its identity—such as wearing a hat, if you are a man. The question now arises: given two individual things belonging to the same species, do they always differ in essence, or is it possible for the essence to be exactly the same in both? Saint Thomas holds the latter view as regards material substances, the former as regards those that are immaterial. Duns Scotus holds that there are *always* differences of essence between two different individual things. (HWP 467)

J

JAMES, WILLIAM

I think it may be wagered that no one except William James has ever lived who would have thought of comparing Hegelianism to a seaside boarding-house. In 1884 this article had no effect, because Hegelianism was still on the up-grade, and philosophers had not learnt to admit that their temperaments had anything to do with their opinions. In 1912 (the date of the reprint) the atmosphere had changed through many causes—among others the influence of William James upon his pupils. I cannot claim to have known him more than superficially except from his writings, but it seems to me that one may distinguish three strands in his nature, all of which contributed to form his outlook. Last in time but first in its philosophical manifestations was the influence of his training in physiology and medicine, which gave him a scientific and slightly materialistic bias as compared to purely literary philosophers who derived their inspiration from Plato, Aristotle, and Hegel. This strand dominated his *Psychology* except in a few crucial passages, such as his discussion of free will. The second element of his philosophic make-up was a mystical and religious bias inherited from his father and shared with his brother. This inspired the *Will to Believe* and his interest in psychical research. Thirdly, there was an attempt, made with all the earnestness of a New England conscience, to exterminate the natural fastidiousness which he also shared with his brother, and replace it by democratic sentiment a la Walt Whitman. (SE 59-60)

JEALOUSY
Jealousy is, of course, a special form of envy: envy of love. The old often envy the young; when they do, they are apt to treat them cruelly. (WIB 76)

JOHN SCOTUS
John supported free will, and this might have passed uncensored; but what roused indignation was the purely philosophic character of his argument. Not that he professed to controvert anything accepted in theology, but that he maintained the equal, or even superior, authority of a philosophy independent of revelation. He contended that reason and revelation are both sources of truth, and therefore cannot conflict; but if they ever *seem* to conflict, reason is to be preferred. (HWP 403)

JUDGMENT, ANALYTIC
The notion that all *a priori* truths are analytic is essentially connected with the doctrine of subject and predicate. An analytic judgment is one in which the predicate is contained in the subject. The subject is supposed defined by a number of predicates, one or more of which are singled out for predication in an analytic judgment. (PL 17)

JUSTICE

But in seeking justice by means of elaborate systems we have been in danger of forgetting that justice alone is not enough. Daily joys, times of liberation from care, adventure, and opportunity for creative activities, are at least as important as justice in bringing about a life that men can feel to be worth living. (AAI 121)

Only justice can give security; and by "justice" I mean the recognition of the equal claims of all human beings. (WIB 72)

K

KANT

Although he had been brought up as a pietist, he was a Liberal both in politics and in theology; he sympathized with the French Revolution until the Reign of Terror, and was a believer in democracy. His philosophy, as we shall see, allowed an appeal to the heart against the cold dictates of theoretical reason, which might with a little exaggeration, be regarded as a pedantic version of the Savoyard Vicar. His principle that every man is to be regarded as an end in himself is a form of the doctrine of the Rights of Man; and his love of freedom is shown in his saying (about children as well as adults) that "there can be nothing more dreadful than that the actions of a man should be subject to the will of another." (HWP 705)

KEPLER

Kepler's great achievement was the discovery of his three laws of planetary motion. Two of these he published in 1609, and the third in 1619. His first law states: The planets describe elliptic orbits, of which the sun occupies one focus. His second law states: The line joining a planet to the sun sweeps out equal areas in equal times. His third law states: The square of the period of revolution of a planet is proportioned to the cube of its average distance from the sun. (HWP 530)

KLEPTOMANIA

Kleptomania consists of stealing things, which often the thief does not really want, in circumstances where he is pretty sure to be caught. It has as a rule some psychological source: the kleptomaniac, unconsciously to himself, is stealing love, or objects having some sexual significance. Kleptomania cannot be dealt with by punishment, but only by psychological understanding. (ESO 36)

KNOW

On the whole, I prefer to use the word "know" in a sense which implies that the knowing is different from what is known, and to accept the consequence that, as a rule, we do not know our present experiences. (IMT 59)

KNOWING

This objective way of viewing knowledge is, to my mind, much more fruitful than the way which has been customary in philosophy. I mean that, if we wish to give a definition of "knowing", we ought to define it as a manner of reacting to the environment, not as involving something (a "state of mind") which only the person who has the knowledge can observe. (OP 17)

KNOWLEDGE

"Knowledge," in my opinion, is a much less precise concept than is generally thought, and has its roots more deeply embedded in unverbalized animal behavior than most philosophers have been willing to admit. The logically basic assumptions to which our analysis leads us are psychologically the end of a long series of refinements which starts from habits of expectations in animals, such as that what has a certain kind of smell will be good to eat. To ask, therefore, whether we "know" the postulates of scientific inference is not so definite a question as it seems. The answer must be: in one sense, yes, in another sense, no; but in the sense in which "no" is the right answer we know nothing whatever, and "knowledge" in this sense is a delusive vision. The perplexities of philosophers are due, in a large measure, to their unwillingness to awaken from this blissful dream. (HK xv-xvi)

"Knowledge," is a vague concept for two reasons. First because the meaning of a word is always more or less vague except in logic and pure mathematics; and second, because all that we count as knowledge is in a greater or less degree uncertain, and there is no way of deciding how much uncertainty makes a belief unworthy to be called "knowledge," any more than how much loss of hair makes a man bald. (HK 98)

L

LANGUAGE

Language has two interconnected merits: first, that it is social, and second, that it supplies public expression for "thoughts" which would otherwise remain private. Without language, or some prelinguistic analogue, our knowledge of the environment is confined to what our own senses have shown us, together with such inferences as our congenital constitution may prompt; but by the help of speech we are able to know what others can relate, and to relate what is no longer sensibly present but only remembered. (HK 59)

The essence of language lies, not in the use of this or that special means of communication, but in the employment of fixed associations (however these may have originated) in order that something now sensible—a spoken word, a picture, a gesture, or what not—may call up the "idea" of something else. Whenever this is done, what is now sensible may be called a "sign" or "symbol," and that of which it is intended to call up the "idea" may be called its "meaning." (AM 191)

LAW, PERIODIC

The elements can be arranged in a series by means of what is called their "atomic weight." By chemical methods, we can remove one element from a compound and replace it by an equal number of atoms of another element; we can observe how much this alters the weight of the compound, and thus we can compare the weight of one kind of atom with the weight of another. (ABCA 14)

LAW, RESPECT FOR

If the method of sanctions is to be used effectively, the sentiment behind it must be respect for law, not love of peace. It is true that, if respect for international law were sufficiently strong, peace would result in the long run; but it would result in consequence of a series of wars from which pacifists would shrink. Respect for law may inspire a wish to punish the criminal, and may thus afford an incentive to war; but love of peace, if used as an incentive to war, produces an inner conflict which is likely to prevent effective action. (WWP 75)

LAW, RULE OF

Means must be found of subjecting the relations of nations to the rule of law, so that a single nation will no longer be, as at present, the judge of its own cause. If this is not done, the world will quickly return to barbarism. (ISOS 40)

The only escape is to have the greatest possible number of disputes settled by legal process and not by a trial of strength. Thus, here again the preservation of internal liberty and external control go hand in hand, and both equally depend upon what is *prima facie* a restraint upon liberty, namely an extension of the domain of law and of the public force necessary for its enforcement. (ISOS 42)

LAZINESS

But I have hopes of laziness as a gospel. I think that if our education were strenuously directed to that end, by men with all the fierce energy produced by our present creed and way of life, it might be possible to induce people to be lazy. I do not mean that no one should work at all, but that few people should work more than is necessary for getting a living. (LAM 117)

LEARN, THE WISH TO

The spontaneous wish to learn, which every normal child possesses, as shown in its efforts to walk and talk, should be the driving-force in education. The substitution of this driving-force for the rod is one of the great advances of our time. (EEC 42)

LEISURE, USE OF

It will be said that, while a little leisure is pleasant, men would not know how to fill their days if they had only four hours of work out of the twenty-four. In so far as this is true in the modern world, it is a condemnation of our civilization; it would not have been true at any earlier period. There was formerly a capacity for light-heartedness and play which has been to some extent inhibited by the cult of efficiency. The modern man thinks that everything ought to be done for the sake of something else, and never for its own sake. (IPI 28)

LIBERALISM

Political change throughout the century was inspired by two systems of thought, Liberalism and Radicalism. Of these, Liberalism was eighteenth-century in origin, and had inspired the American and French Revolutions. It stood for liberty, both individual and national, with as little government as possible; indeed, the functions of government were reduced by many Liberals to the prevention of crime. In agricultural communities it was successful in producing stable conditions and a fairly contented population; but it had little to offer to industrial wage-earners, since its philosophy suggested no way of curbing economic power in the hands of individuals. It succeeded in establishing Parliaments, with a greater or less degree of power, in every country of Europe and America, as well as in Japan and China; but the resultant benefits were, in many parts of the world, not very noticeable. (FO 447-8)

This is the essential difference between the Liberal outlook and that of the totalitarian State, that the former regards the welfare of the State as residing ultimately in the welfare of the individual, while the latter regards the State as the end and individuals merely as indispensable ingredients, whose welfare must be subordinated to a mystical totality which is a cloak for the interests of the rulers (P 302-3)

LIBERALISM, ESSENCE OF

In general, important civilizations start with a rigid and superstitious system, gradually relaxed, and leading, at a certain stage, to a period of brilliant genius, while the good of the old tradition remains and the evil inherent in its dissolution has not yet developed. But as the evil unfolds, it leads to anarchy, thence, inevitably, to a new tyranny, producing a new synthesis secured by a new system of dogma. The doctrine of liberalism is an attempt to escape from this endless oscillation. The essence of liberalism is an attempt to secure a social order not based on irrational dogma, and insuring stability without involving more restraints than are necessary for the preservation of the community. Whether this attempt can succeed only the future can determine. (HWP xxiii)

LIBERTY

The liberty of the individual should be respected where his actions do not directly, obviously, and indubitably do harm to other people. Otherwise our persecuting instincts will produce a stereotyped society as in sixteenth-century Spain. The danger is real and pressing. (SE 186)

"Liberty" is a good watchword, but it is not sufficient as an international principle. There should be liberty to do certain kinds of things, but not certain other kinds. Primarily, there should be no liberty to make aggressive war. It is obvious that this requires some supernational authority with a preponderance of armed forces and with a judicial body entrusted with the duty of pronouncing quickly whether, in a given case, aggression has taken place. (PPW 88)

LIFE, ATTITUDES TOWARD

The three attitudes most prevalent in people's philosophy are the practical, the mystical, and the scientific. Each is insufficient as covering the whole of life; each becomes fallacious when it tries to extend beyond its proper sphere. The practical attitude asks: "What shall I do?" The mystical attitude asks: "What shall I feel?" The scientific attitude asks: "What shall I believe, or what can I know?" (TWW 11)

LIFE, MAN'S TRUE

Man's true life does not consist in the business of filling his belly and clothing his body, but in art and thought and love, in the creation and contemplation of beauty and in the scientific understanding of the world. If the world is to be regenerated, it is in these things not only in material goods, that all must be enabled to participate. (PIC 40-1)

LOCKE

A characteristic of Locke, which descended from him to the whole Liberal movement, is lack of dogmatism. Some few certainties he takes over from his predecessors: our own existence, the existence of God, and the truth of mathematics. But wherever his doctrines differ from those of his forerunners, they are to the effect that truth is hard to ascertain, and that a rational man will hold his opinions with some measure of doubt. This temper of mind is obviously connected with religious toleration, with the success of parliamentary democracy, with *laissez-faire*, and with the whole system of liberal maxims. Although he is a deeply religious man, a devout believer in Christianity who accepts revelation as a source of knowledge, he nevertheless hedges round professed revelations with rational safeguards. (HWP 606-7)

LOGIC

Activity can supply only one half of wisdom; the other half depends upon receptive passivity. Ultimately, the controversy between those who base logic upon "truth" and those who base it upon "inquiry" arises from a difference of values, and cannot be argued without, at some point, begging the question. (DNL 156)

In logic, it is a waste of time to deal with inferences concerning particular cases: we deal throughout with completely general and purely formal implications, leaving it to other sciences to discover when the hypotheses are verified and when they are not. (KEW 47)

Although we can no longer be satisfied to define logical propositions as those that follow from the law of contradiction, we can and must still admit that they are a wholly different class of propositions from those that we come to know empirically. They all have the characteristic which, a moment ago, we agreed to call "tautology." This, combined with the fact that they can be expressed wholly in terms of variables and logical constants (a logical constant being something which remains constant in a proposition even when all its constituents are changed)—will give the definition of logic or pure mathematics. (IMP 204-5)

LOGICAL ATOMISM

I hold that logic is what is fundamental in philosophy, and that schools should be characterized rather by their logic than by their metaphysic. My own logic is atomic, and it is this aspect upon which I should wish to lay stress. Therefore I prefer to describe my philosophy as "logical atomism," rather than as "realism," whether with or without some prefixed adjective. (LA 359)

The third type, which may be called "logical atomism" for want of a better name, has gradually crept into philosophy through the critical scrutiny of mathematics. This type of philosophy, which is the one that I wish to advocate, has not as yet many whole-hearted adherents, but the "new realism" which owes its inception to Harvard is very largely impregnated with its spirit. It represents, I believe, the same kind of advance as was introduced into physics by Galileo: the substitution of piecemeal, detailed, and verifiable results for large untested generalities recommended only by a certain appeal to imagination. (KEW 4)

LOVE

Love is a word which covers a variety of feelings; I have used it purposely, as I wish to include them all. Love as an emotion—which is what I am speaking about, for love "on principle" does not seem to me genuine—moves between two poles: on the one side, pure delight in contemplation; on the other, pure benevolence. (WIB 22)

LOVE, INCULCATION OF

Love cannot exist as a duty: to tell a child that it *ought* to love its parents and its brothers and sisters is utterly useless, if not worse. Parents who wish to be loved must behave so as to elicit love, and must try to give to their children those physical and mental characteristics which produce expansive affections. (EEC 188)

M

MACHIAVELLI

His most famous work, *The Prince,* was written in 1513, and dedicated to Lorenzo the Magnificent, since he hoped (vainly, as it proved) to win the favour of the Medici. Its tone is perhaps partly due to this practical purpose; his longer work, the *Discourses,* which he was writing at the same time, is markedly more republican and more liberal. He says at the beginning of *The Prince* that he will not speak of republics in this book, since he has dealt with them elsewhere. Those who do not read also the *Discourses* are likely to get a very one-sided view of his doctrine. (HWP 505)

MAJORITY, POWER OF THE

I think it must be admitted that, if any important economic change is to be successfully carried out, a government will need some years of free initiative. This, however, is not incompatible with democracy, which consists in the occasional exercise of popular control, but does not demand the constant hampering of the executive. The ultimate power of the majority is very important to minimize the harshness inevitably involved in great changes, and to prevent a rapidity of transformation which causes a revulsion of feeling. I do not believe, therefore, that an authoritarian government is better than a democracy, though I believe that, in times of crisis, a strong and temporarily unhampered executive is necessary. (FOD 381)

MAN, GOAL OF

Mankind has become so much one family that we cannot insure our own prosperity except by insuring that of everyone else. If you wish to be happy yourself, you must resign yourself to seeing others also happy. Whether science can continue, and whether, while it continues, it can do more good than harm, depends upon the capacity of mankind to learn this simple lesson. Perhaps it is necessary that all should learn it, but it must be learned by all who have great power, and among those some still have a long way to go. (STS 33)

MAN, THE HAPPY

The happy man is the man who lives objectively, who has free affections and wide interests, who secures his happiness through these interests and affections and through the fact that they, in turn, make him an object of interest and affection to many others. (CH 244)

MAN, THE PURPOSE OF

We, too, in all our deeds, bear our part in a process of which we cannot guess the development: even the obscurest are actors in a drama of which we know that it is great. Whether any purpose that we value will be achieved, we cannot tell; but the drama itself, in any case, is full of Titanic grandeur. This quality it is the business of the historian to extract from the bewildering multitude of irrelevant details. (OH 214)

MANICHAEISM

Manichaeism combined Christian and Zoroastrian elements, teaching that evil is a positive principle, embodied in matter, while the good principle is embodied in spirit. It condemned meat-eating, and all sex, even in marriage. (HWP 325)

MANKIND

The whole world of art and literature and learning is international; what is done in one country is not done for that country, but for mankind. If we ask ourselves what are the things that raise mankind above the brutes, what are the things that make us think the human race more valuable than any species of animals, we shall find that none of them are things in which any one nation can have exclusive property, but all are things in which the whole world can share. Those who have any care for these things, those who wish to see mankind fruitful in the work which men alone can do, will take little account of national boundaries, and have little care to what state a man happens to owe allegiance. (PI 166-7)

MAN'S POWER

Brief and powerless is Man's life; on him and all his race the slow, sure doom falls pitiless and dark. Blind to good and evil, reckless of destruction, omnipotent matter rolls on its relentless way; for Man, condemned to-day to lose his dearest, to-morrow himself to pass through the gate of darkness, it remains only to cherish, ere yet the blow falls, the lofty thoughts that ennoble his little day; disdaining the coward terrors of the slave of Fate, to worship at the shrine that his own hands have built; undismayed by the empire of chance, to preserve a mind free from the wanton tyranny that rules his outward life; proudly defiant of the irresistible forces that tolerate, for a moment, his knowledge and his condemnation, to sustain alone, a weary but unyielding Atlas, the world that his own ideals have fashioned despite the trampling march of unconscious power. (ML 56-7)

MARRIAGE

It is therefore possible for a civilized man and woman to be happy in marriage, although if this is to be the case a number of conditions must be fulfilled. There must be a feeling of complete equality on both sides; there must be no interference with mutual freedom; there must be the most complete physical and mental intimacy; and there must be a certain similarity in regards to standards of values. (It is fatal, for example, if one values only money while the other values only good work.) Given all these conditions, I believe marriage to be the best and most important relation that can exist between two human beings. (MM 143)

MARRIAGE, DISSOLUTION OF

To the eye of the sane maker of laws it would seem that the special contract of partnership known as marriage should be dissolved altogether when it has failed in its object and when the partners are no longer carrying on business together, but living separate (subject always to the one special difficulty of the partnership assets which have been created in the shape of children). . . . (WMD 134)

MARRIAGE, THE NEW IDEAL OF

I doubt if there is any radical core except in some form of religion, so firmly and sincerely believed in as to dominate even the life of instinct. The individual is not the end and aim of his own being: outside the individual, there is the community, the future of mankind, the immensity of the universe in which all our hopes and fears are a mere pinpoint. A man and woman with reverence for the spirit of life in each other, with an equal sense of their own unimportance beside the whole life of man, may become comrades without interference with liberty, and may achieve the union of instinct without doing violence to the life of mind and spirit. As religion dominated the old form of marriage, so religion must dominate the new. But it must be a new religion, based upon liberty, justice and love, not upon authority and law and hell-fire. (MPQ 461)

MARSIGLIO

Marsiglio of Padua (1270-1342), on the contrary, inaugurated the new form of opposition to the Pope, in which the Emperor has mainly a role of decorative dignity. He was a close friend of William of Occam, whose political opinions he influenced. Politically, he is more important than Occam. He holds that the legislator is the majority of the people, and that the majority has the right to punish princes. He applies popular sovereignty also to the Church, and he includes the laity. (HWP 470)

MARX

Considered purely as a philosopher, Marx has grave shortcomings. He is too practical, too much wrapped up in the problems of his time. His purview is confined to this planet, and, within this planet, to Man. Since Copernicus, it has been evident that Man has not the cosmic importance which he formerly arrogated to himself. No man who has failed to assimilate this fact has a right to call his philosophy scientific. (HWP 788)

MASS

When we substitute space-time for time, we find that the measured mass (as opposed to the proper mass) is a quantity of the same kind as the momentum in a given direction; it might be called the momentum in the time direction. The measured mass is obtained by multiplying the invariant mass by the *time* traversed in traveling through unit interval; the momentum is obtained by multiplying the same invariant mass by the *distance* traversed (in the given direction) in traveling through unit interval. (ABCR 152)

MATERIALISTS
Those who argue that matter is the reality and mind a mere property of protoplasm are called "materialists." They have been rare among philosophers, but common, at certain periods, among men of science. (AM 10)

MATHEMATICAL LOGIC
The new philosophy is not merely critical. It is constructive, but as science is constructive, bit by bit and tentatively. It has a special technical method of construction, namely, mathematical logic, a new branch of mathematics, much more akin to philosophy than any of the traditional branches. Mathematical logic makes it possible, as it never was before, to see what is the outcome, for philosophy, of a given body of scientific doctrine, what entities must be assumed, and what relations between them. (SE 74)

MATHEMATICS AND PHILOSOPHY
The principles of mathematics have always had an important relation to philosophy. Mathematics apparently contains *a priori* knowledge of a high degree of certainty, and most philosophy aspires to *a priori* knowledge. Ever since Zeno the Eleatic, philosophers of an idealistic caste have sought to throw discredit on mathematics by manufacturing contradictions which were designed to show that mathematicians had not arrived at real metaphysical truth,

and that the philosophers were able to supply a better brand. There is a great deal of this in Kant, and still more in Hegel. (SE 73)

MATTER

A piece of matter, as it is known empirically, is not a single existing thing, but a system of existing things. When several people simultaneously see the same table, they all see something different; therefore "the" table, which they are all supposed to see, must be either a hypothesis or a construction. "The" table is to be neutral as between different observers: it does not favour the aspect seen by one man at the expense of that seen by another. (AM 97)

The main point for the philosophers in the modern theory is the disappearance of matter as a "thing". It has been replaced by emanations from a locality—the sort of influences that characterise haunted rooms in ghost stories. As we shall see in the next chapter, the theory of relativity leads to a similar destruction of the solidity of matter, by a different line of argument. All sorts of events happen in the physical world, but tables and chairs, the sun and moon, and even our daily bread, have become pale abstractions, mere laws exhibited in the successions of events which radiate from certain regions. (OP 106)

The word matter is, in philosophy, the name of a problem. Assuming that, in perception, we are assured of the existence of something other than ourselves—an assumption which, as we saw in the last chapter, Leibniz made on very inadequate grounds—the question inevitably arises: of what nature is this something external to ourselves? In so far as it appears to be in space, we name it matter. (PL 75)

MEANING

It is common to distinguish two aspects, meaning and denotation, in such phrases as "the author of Waverley." The meaning will be a certain complex, consisting (at least) of authorship and Waverley with some relation; the denotation will be Scott. (ML 223-4)

When through the law of conditioned reflexes, A has come to be a cause of C, we will call A an "associative" cause of C, and C an "associative" effect of A. We shall say that, to a given person, the word A, when he hears it, "means" C, if the associative effects of A are closely similar to those of C; and we shall say that the word A, when he utters it, "means" C, if the utterance of A is an associative effect of C, or of something previously associated with C. To put the matter more concretely, the word "Peter" means a certain person if the associated effects of hearing the word "Peter" are closely similar to those of seeing Peter, and the associative causes of uttering the word "Peter" are occurrences previously associated with Peter. Of course as our experience increases in complexity this simple schema becomes obscured and overlaid, but I think it remains fundamentally true. (OP 52)

MEANS

Men who boast of being what is called "practical" are for the most part exclusively preoccupied with means. But theirs is only one-half of wisdom. When we take account of the other half, which is concerned with ends, the economic process and the whole of human life take on an entirely new aspect. (AAI 115)

MEDIEVAL WORLD

The medieval world, as contrasted with the world of antiquity, is characterized by various forms of dualism. There is the dualism of clergy and laity, the dualism of Latin and Teuton, the dualism of the kingdom of God and the kingdoms of this world, the dualism of the spirit and the flesh. All these are exemplified in the dualism of Pope and Emperor. (HWP 302)

MEMORY

True memory, which we must now endeavour to understand, consists of knowledge of past events, but not of all such knowledge. Some knowledge of past events, for example what we learn through reading history, is on a par with knowledge we can acquire concerning the future; it is obtained by inference, not (so to speak) spontaneously. (AM 172-3)

The first extension beyond sense-data to be considered is acquaintance by memory. It is obvious that we often remember what we have seen or heard or had otherwise present to our senses, and that in such cases we are still immediately aware of what we remember, in spite of the fact that it appears as past and not as present. (PP 76)

MENTAL

My own belief is that the "mental" and the "physical" are not so disparate as is generally thought. I should define a "mental" occurrence as one which someone knows otherwise than by inference; the distinction between "mental" and "physical" therefore belongs to theory of knowledge, not to metaphysics. (HK 209)

The definition of the term "mental" is more difficult, and can only be satisfactorily given after many difficult controversies have been discussed and decided. For present purposes therefore I must content myself with assuming a dogmatic answer to these controversies. I shall call a particular "mental" when it is aware of something, and I shall call a fact "mental" when it contains a mental particular as a constituent. (ML 150)

MICHELSON-MORLEY EXPERIMENT

On the face of it, and apart from hypotheses *ad hoc*, the Michelson-Morley experiment (in conjunction with others) showed that, relatively to the earth, the velocity of light is the same in all directions, and that this is equally true at all times of the year, although the direction of the earth's motion is always changing as it goes round the sun. (ABCR 33)

MILL, JAMES

Mill had become a Radical before he met Bentham; in psychology he was a disciple of Hartley, in economics he accepted Malthus and was a close friend of Ricardo, in politics he was an extreme democrat and a doctrinaire believer in *laissez faire.* He was not an original thinker, but he was clear and vigorous, and had the unquestioning faith of the born disciple, with the disciple's utter contempt for doctrines at variance with the Master's. "I see clearly enough what poor Kant is about," he wrote, after a brief attempt to read that philosopher. Like all his kind, he greatly admired Helvetius, from whom he accepted the current doctrine of the omnipotence of education. (FO 94)

MIND

Out of habit, the peculiarities of what we call "mind" can be constructed; a mind is a track of sets of compresent events in a region of space-time where there is matter which is peculiarly liable to form habits. The greater the liability, the more complex and organized the mind becomes. Thus a mind and a brain are not really distinct, but when we speak of a mind we are thinking chiefly of the set of compresent events in the region concerned, and of their several relations to other events forming parts of other periods in the history of the spatio-temporal tube which we are considering, whereas when we speak of the brain we are taking the set of compresent events as a whole, and considering its external relations to other sets of compresent events, also taken as wholes; in a word, we are considering the shape of the tube, not the events of which each cross-section of it is composed. (LA 382)

Thus "mind" and "mental" are merely approximate concepts, giving a convenient shorthand for certain approximate laws. In a completed science, the word "mind" and the word "matter" would both disappear, and would be replaced by causal laws concerning "events", the only events known to us otherwise than in their mathematical and causal properties being percepts, which are events situated in the same region as a brain and having effects of a peculiar sort called "knowledge-reactions." (OP 281)

MINORITIES

Where race questions are not involved, a sufficiently determined minority will generally be able to hold its own against the state so far as its own affairs are concerned. It is in the highest degree desirable that this should be possible, and a state which treats minorities ruthlessly is *pro tanto* a bad state. (PIC 200)

MINORITY, NON-GEOGRAPHICAL

The question of minorities that are not geographically concentrated is more difficult. The most prominent example, of course, is that of the Jews. I think the international authority ought to forbid any legal discrimination against any minority group, with the exception of political groups aiming at treason against their national government or against the world federation. (FOP 11)

MNEMIC PHENOMENA

Following a suggestion derived from Semon (*Die Mneme*, Leipzig, 1904; 2nd edition, 1908, English translation, Allen & Unwin, 1921; *Die mnemischen Empfindungen*, Leipzig, 1909), we will give the name of "mnemic phenomena" to those responses of an organism which, so far as hitherto observed facts are concerned, can only be brought under causal laws by including past occurrences in the history of the organism as part of the causes of the present response. (AM 78)

MODERATION

The ancients, however, were clearly in the right. In the good life there must be a balance between different activities, and no one of them must be carried so far as to make the others impossible. The gormandizer sacrifices all other pleasures to that of eating, and by so doing diminishes the total happiness of his life. (CH 166)

MODESTY

Modesty is considered a virtue, but for my part I am very doubtful whether, in its more extreme forms, it deserves to be so regarded. Modest people need a great deal of reassuring, and often do not dare to attempt tasks which they are quite capable of performing. Modest people believe themselves to be outshone by those with whom they habitually associate. They are therefore particularly prone to envy, and, through envy, to unhappiness and ill will. For my part, I think there is much to be said for bringing up a boy to think himself a fine fellow. (CH 89)

MONOPHYSITE HERESY

In 449, after the death of Saint Cyril, a synod at Ephesus tried to carry the triumph further, and thereby fell into the heresy opposite to that of Nestorius; this is called the Monophysite heresy, and maintains that Christ has only one nature. (HWP 369)

MORALITY

On the whole, I think that, speaking philosophically, all acts ought to be judged by their effects; but as this is difficult and uncertain and takes time, it is desirable, in practice, that some kinds of acts should be condemned and others praised without waiting to investigate consequences. I should say, therefore, with the utilitarians, that the right act, in any given circumstances, is that which, on the data, will probably produce the greatest balance of good over evil of all the acts that are possible; but that the performance of such acts may be promoted by the existence of a moral code. (P 246)

MORALITY, CIVIC AND PERSONAL

Throughout recorded history, ethical beliefs have had two very different sources, one political, the other concerned with personal religious and moral convictions. In the Old Testament the two appear quite separately, one as the Law, the other as the Prophets. In the Middle Ages there was the same kind of distinction between the official morality inculcated by the hierarchy and the personal holiness that was taught and practised by the great mystics. This duality of personal and civic morality, which still persists, is one of which any adequate ethical theory must take account. Without civic morality communities perish; without personal morality their survival has no value. Therefore civic and personal morality are equally necessary to a good world. (AAI 110-1)

MORALS, RELATIVITY IN

There is also, in all conventional moralists, a gross ignorance of psychology, making them unable to realize that certain virtues imply certain correlated vices, so that in recommending a virtue the consideration which ought to weigh is: does this virtue, with its correlative vice, outweigh the opposite virtue with its correlative vice? The fact that a virtue is good in itself is not enough; it is necessary to take account of the vices that it entails and the virtues that it excludes. (PIC 161)

MORE'S UTOPIA

More's *Utopia* was in many ways astonishingly liberal. I am not thinking so much of the preaching of communism, which was in the tradition of many religious movements. I am thinking of what is said about war, about religion, and religious toleration, against the wanton killing of animals (there is a most eloquent passage against hunting) and in favour of a mild criminal law. (The book opens with an argument against the death penalty for death.) It must be admitted, however, that life in More's Utopia, as in most others, would be intolerably dull. Diversity is essential to happiness, and in Utopia there is hardly any. This is a defect of all planned social systems, actual as well as imaginary. (HWP 521-2)

MYSTICAL ATTITUDE TOWARD LIFE

The mystical attitude is best expressed in the religions of India, although it is also found in Christian mysticism, and in Greek philosophy even before the time of Socrates. It is based almost always on a certain definite experience, the mystical experience. The distinctive feature of the whole thing is emotion. The beliefs it inspires are often bad ones, but the feelings are good ones. (TWW 13)

MYSTICISM

I believe that, when the mystics contrast "reality" with "appearance," the word "reality" has not a logical, but an emotional significance: it means what is, in some sense, important. When it is said that time is "unreal," what should be said is that, in some sense and on some occasions, it is important to conceive the universe as a whole, as the Creator, if He existed, must have conceived it in deciding to create it. When so conceived, all process is within one completed whole: past, present, and future all exist, in some sense, together, and the present does not have that pre-eminent reality which it has to our usual ways of apprehending the world. If this interpretation is accepted, mysticism expresses an emotion, not a fact; it does not assert anything, and therefore can be neither confirmed nor contradicted by science. The fact that mystics do make assertions is owing to their inability to separate emotional importance from scientific validity. It is, of course, not to be expected that they will accept this view, but it is the only one, so far as I can see, which, while admitting something of their claim, is not repugnant to the scientific intelligence. (RAS 194-5)

N

NAME

... a *name*, which is a simple symbol, directly designating an individual which is its meaning, and having this meaning in its own right, independently of the meaning of all other words. (IMP 174)

NAME, PROPER

To speak for the moment in terms of physics, we give proper names to certain continuous stretches of space-time, such as Socrates, France, or the moon. In former days, it would have been said that we give a proper name to a substance or collection of substances, but now we have to find a different phrase to express the object of a proper name. (IMT 38)

NAMES, GENERAL

Passing on from proper names, we come next to general names, such as "man," "cat," "triangle." A word such as "man" means a whole class of such collections of particulars as have proper names. The several members of the class are assembled together in virtue of some similarity or common property. (AM 194)

NAPOLEON

In Germany, feeling about Napoleon was more divided. There were those who, like Heine, saw him as the mighty missionary of liberalism, the destroyer of serfdom, the enemy of legitimacy; the man who made hereditary princelings tremble; there were others who saw him as Antichrist, the would-be destroyer of the noble German nation, the immoralist who had proved once for all that Teutonic virtue can only be preserved by unquenchable hatred of France. Bismarck effected a synthesis: Napoleon remained Antichrist, but an Antichrist to be imitated, not merely to be abhorred. Nietzsche, who accepted the compromise, remarked with ghoulish joy that the classical age of war is coming, and that we owe this boon, not to the French Revolution, but to Napoleon. And in this way nationalism, Satanism, and hero-worship, the legacy of Byron, became part of the complex soul of Germany. (HWP 751-2)

NATION

What constitutes a nation is a sentiment and an instinct, a sentiment of similarity and an instinct of belonging to the same group or herd. (PI 148)

NATIONALISM

The inevitable outcome of the doctrine that each nation should have unrestricted sovereignty is to compel the citizens of each nation to engage in irksome activities and to incur sacrifices, often of life itself, in order to thwart the designs of other nations. (FAG 258)

Nationalism is a development of herd-instinct, it is the habit of taking as one's herd the nation to which one belongs. As to what constitutes a nation, the only thing that can be said definitely is that a nation is a group which is defined geographically. (PIC 16)

NEEDS, OUR AGE'S

There are certain things that our age needs, and certain things that it should avoid. It needs compassion and a wish that mankind should be happy; it needs the desire for knowledge and the determination to eschew pleasant myths; it needs, above all, courageous hope and the impulse to creativeness. The things that it must avoid and that have brought it to the brink of catastrophe are cruelty, envy, greed, competitiveness, search for irrational subjective certainty, and what Freudians call the death wish. (ISOS 59)

NESTORIANISM

Saint Cyril was pained to learn that Constantinople was being led astray by the teaching of its patriarch Nestorius, who maintained that there were two persons in Christ, one human and one divine. On this ground Nestorius objected to the new practice of calling the Virgin "Mother of God"; she was, he said, only the mother of the human Person, while the divine Person, who was God, had no mother. (HWP 368)

NEUTRAL-MONISM

I shall try to persuade you in the course of these lectures that matter is not so material and mind not so mental as is generally supposed. When we are speaking of matter, it will seem as if we were inclining to idealism; when we are speaking of mind, it will seem as if we were inclining to materialism. Neither is the truth. Our world is to be constructed out of what the American realists call "neutral" entities which have neither the hardness and indestructibility of matter, nor the reference to objects which is supposed to characterize mind. (AM 36)

NEWTON

Newton (1642-1727) achieved the final and complete triumph for which Copernicus, Kepler, and Galileo had prepared the way. Starting from his three laws of motion—of which the first two are due to Galileo—he proved that Kepler's three laws are equivalent to the proposition that every planet, at every moment, has an acceleration towards the sun which varies inversely as the square of the distance from the sun. He showed that accelerations towards the earth and the sun, following the same formula, explain the moon's motion, and that the acceleration of falling bodies on the earth's surface is again related to that of the moon according to the inverse square law. He defined "force" as the change of motion, i.e., of acceleration. He was thus able to enunciate his law of universal gravitation: "Every body attracts every other with a force directly proportional to the product of their masses, and inversely proportional to the square of the distance between them." From this formula he was able to deduce everything in planetary theory: the motions of the planets and their satellites, the orbits of comets, the tides. It appeared later that even the minute departures from elliptical orbits on the part of the planets were deducible from Newton's law. The triumph was so complete that Newton was in danger of becoming another Aristotle, and imposing an insuperable barrier to progress. In England, it was not till a century after his death that men freed themselves from his authority sufficiently to do important original work in the subjects of which he had treated. (HWP 535)

NIETZSCHE

Nietzsche (1844-1900) regarded himself, rightly, as the successor of Schopenhauer, to whom, however, he is superior in many ways, particularly in the consistency and coherence of his doctrine. Schopenhauer's oriental ethic of renunciation seems out of harmony with his metaphysic of the omnipotence of will; in Nietzsche, the will has ethical as well as metaphysical primacy. Nietzsche, though a professor, was a literary rather than an academic philosopher. He invented no new technical theories in ontology or epistemology; his importance is primarily in ethics, and secondarily as an acute historical critic. (HWP 760)

NON-VIOLENCE

The doctrine of non-violence, which has been practised on a large scale in India, can be defended on other than religious grounds. In certain circumstances, it is the best practical policy. These circumstances arise when one party is unarmed but resolute, while the opposing party is armed but irresolute. Killing people who do not resist is a disgusting business, and decent men will yield much, rather than persist in it. But when the enemy is resolute and brutal the method has no success. The Church persecuted heretics and Jews relentlessly, even when they made no attempt at armed resistance. The Japanese, if they conquered India, would make short work of any movement of non-cooperation on the part of Gandhi's followers. Absolute pacifism, therefore, as a method of gaining your ends, is subject to very severe limitations. (FOP 7-8)

O

OBJECT, PHYSICAL

The real table, if it exists, we will call a "physical object." (PP 18)

OBJECTIVITY

When two people simultaneously have percepts which they regard as belonging to one group, if the inferences of the one differ from those of the other, one of them at least must be drawing false inferences, and must therefore have an element of subjectivity in his perception. It is only where the inferences of the two observers agree that both perceptions may be objective. It will be seen that, according to this view, the objectivity of a perception does not depend only upon what it is in itself, but also upon the experience of the percipient. (AOM 223)

OCCAM'S RAZOR

. . . . . the maxim which inspires all scientific philosophizing, namely "Occam's razor": *Entities are not to be multiplied without necessity.* In other words, in dealing with any subject-matter, find out what entities are undeniably involved, and state everything in terms of these entities. (KEW 113)

OEDIPUS COMPLEX

I do not believe that there is, except in rare morbid cases, an "Oedipus Complex", in the sense of a special attraction of sons to mothers and daughters to fathers. The excessive influence of the parent, where it exists, will belong to the parent who has had most to do with the child—generally the mother—without regard to the difference of sex. Of course, it may happen that a daughter who dislikes her mother and sees little of her father will idealize the latter; but in that case the influence is exerted by dreams, not by the actual father. Idealization consists of hanging hopes to a peg; the peg is merely convenient, and has nothing to do with the nature of the hopes. Undue parental influence is quite a different thing from this, since it is connected with the actual person, not with an imaginary portrait. (EEC 190-1)

OLIGARCHY

The natural successor to absolute monarchy is oligarchy. But oligarchy may be of many sorts; it may be the rule of a hereditary aristocracy, of the rich, or of a church or political party. These produce very different results. A hereditary landed aristocracy is apt to be conservative, proud, stupid, and rather brutal; for these reasons among others, it is always worsted in a struggle with the higher bourgeoisie. A government of the rich prevailed in all the free cities of the Middle Ages, and survived in Venice until Napoleon extinguished it. Such governments have been, on the whole, more enlightened and astute than any others known to history. Venice, in particular, steered a prudent course through centuries of complicated intrigue, and had a diplomatic service far more efficient than that of any other State. (P 186-7)

OMNISCIENCE, FIRST-ORDER AND LIMITED FIRST-ORDER

Let us give the name "first-order omniscience" to knowledge of the truth or falsehood of every sentence not containing general words. "Limited first-order omniscience" will mean similar complete knowledge concerning all sentences of a certain form, say the form "x is human." (HK 133)

ONTOLOGICAL ARGUMENT

The ontological argument will be unsound, and God's existence itself, being contingent, must have a sufficient reason which inclines without necessitating. But if this be required, we might just as well admit the preestablished harmony as an ultimate fact, since the assumption of God's existence is insufficient for its explanation. (PL 188-9)

ONTOLOGICAL ARGUMENT, LATER HISTORY OF THE

This argument has never been accepted by theologians. It was adversely criticized at the time; then it was forgotten till the latter half of the thirteenth century. Thomas Aquinas rejected it, and among theologians his authority has prevailed ever since. But among philosophers it has had a better fate. Descartes revived it in a somewhat amended form; Leibniz thought that it could be made valid by the addition of a supplement to prove that God is *possible.* Kant considered that he had demolished it once and for all. Nevertheless, in some sense, it underlies the system of Hegel, and his followers, and reappears in Bradley's principle: "What may be and must be, is." (HWP 417)

OPEN-MINDEDNESS

But since our intellectual life is only a part of our activity, and since curiosity is perpetually coming into conflict with other passions, there is need of certain intellectual virtues, such as open-mindedness. We become impervious to new truth both from habit and from desire: we find it hard to disbelieve what we have emphatically believed for a number of years, and also what ministers to self-esteem or any other fundamental passion. Open-mindedness should therefore be one of the qualities that education aims at producing. (EEC 77)

OPINION, FREEDOM OF

I admit, the issue of academic freedom is not in itself of the first magnitude. But it is part and parcel of the same battle. Let it be remembered that what is at stake, in the greatest issues as well as in those that seem smaller, is the freedom of the individual human spirit to express its beliefs and hopes for mankind, whether they be shared by many or by few or none. New hopes, new beliefs, and new thoughts are at all times necessary to mankind, and it is not out of a dead uniformity that they can be expected to arise. (FAC 33)

If I had considered only my own interests and inclinations I should have retired at once. But however wise such action might have been from a personal point of view, it would also, in my judgment, have been cowardly and selfish. A great many people who realized that their own interests and the principles of toleration and free speech were at stake were anxious from the first to continue the controversy. If I had retired I should have robbed them of their *casus belli* and tacitly assented to the proposition that substantial groups shall be allowed to drive out of public office individuals whose opinions, race, or nationality they find repugnant. This to me would appear immoral. (LBRC April 26, 1940)

OPPRESSED, VIRTUE OF THE

As appears from the various instances that we have considered, the stage in which superior virtue is attributed to the oppressed is transient and unstable. It begins only when the oppressors come to have a bad conscience, and this only happens when their power is no longer secure. The idealizing of the victim is useful for a time: if virtue is the greatest of goods, and if subjection makes people virtuous, it is kind to refuse them power, since it would destroy their virtue. If it is difficult for a rich man to enter the kingdom of heaven, it is a noble act on his part to keep his wealth and so imperil his eternal bliss for the benefit of his poorer brethren. It was a fine self-sacrifice on the part of men to relieve women of the dirty work of politics. And so on. But sooner or later the oppressed class will argue that its superior virtue is a reason in favor of its having power, and the oppressors will find their own weapons turned against them. (UE 63)

P

PACIFIST, INDIVIDUAL

There is another important distinction, namely, that between individual and political pacifism. The individual pacifist says: No matter what my government may command, I myself will not fight. The political pacifist, on the contrary, is concerned to keep his government out of war. (FOP 8)

PARALLELISM, PSYCHO-PHYSICAL

The modern doctrine of psycho-physical parallelism is not appreciably different from this theory of the Cartesian school. Psycho-physical parallelism is the theory that mental and physical events each have causes in their own sphere, but run on side by side owing to the fact that every state of the brain coexists with a definite state of the mind, and vice versa. This view of the reciprocal causal independence of mind and matter has no basis except in metaphysical theory. (AM 35)

PARENTHOOD, HAPPINESS OF

For my own part, speaking personally, I have found the happiness of parenthood greater than any other that I have experienced. I believe that when circumstances lead men or women to forego this happiness, a very deep need remains ungratified, and that this produces a dissatisfaction and listlessness of which the cause may remain quite unknown. To be happy in this world, especially when youth is past, it is necessary to feel oneself not merely an isolated individual whose day will soon be over, but part of the stream of life flowing on from the first germ to the remote and unknown future. (CH 198)

PARMENIDES

What makes Parmenides historically important is that he invented a form of metaphysical argument that, in one form or another, is to be found in most subsequent metaphysicians down to and including Hegel. He is often said to have invented logic, but what he really invented was metaphysics based on logic. (HWP 48)

PAROCHIALISM

Our age is the most parochial since Homer. I speak not of any geographical parish: the inhabitants of Mudcombe-in-the-Meer are more aware than at any former time of what is being done and thought at Praha, at Gorki, or at Peiping. It is in the chronological sense that we are parochial: as the new names conceal the historic cities of Prague, Nijni-Novgorod, and Pekin, so new catchwords hide from us the thoughts and feelings of our ancestors, even when they differed little from our own. (UE 65)

PASSIONS, COLLECTIVE

Men's collective passions are mainly evil; far the strongest of them are hatred and rivalry directed towards other groups. Therefore at present all that gives men power to indulge their collective passions is bad. That is why science threatens to cause the destruction of civilization. The only solid hope seems to lie in the possibility of world-wide domination by one group, say the United States, leading to the gradual foundation of an orderly economic and political world-government. (I 63)

PATRIOTISM, TRUE

Those of us who do not wish to see our whole civilization go down in red ruin have a great and difficult duty to perform—to guard the door of our minds against patriotism. I mean, that we should view impartially any dispute between our own country and another, that we should teach ourselves not to believe our own country morally superior to others, and that even in time of war we should view the whole matter as a neutral might view it. This is part of the larger duty of pursuing truth; nationalism cannot survive without false beliefs. If we can learn to serve truth, to be truthful in our thoughts, to avoid the flattering myths in which we like to disguise our passions, we shall have done what we can to save our world from disaster. For this creed it is worth-while to suffer, and indeed those who have it must suffer, for persecution is as bitter as in the days of the Spanish Inquisition. But in the very suffering there is happiness, and a promise of better things in the time to come. (PNW 12)

PEACE

Our own planet, in which philosophers are apt to take a parochial and excessive interest, was once too hot to support life, and will in time be too cold. After ages during which the earth produced harmless trilobites and butterflies, evolution progressed to the point at which it generated Neros, Genghis Khans, and Hitlers. This, however, is a passing nightmare; in time the earth will become again incapable of supporting life, and peace will return. (UE 9)

PEACE, PSYCHOLOGY OF

The problem of making peace with our anarchic impulses is one which has been too little studied, but one which becomes more and more imperative as scientific technique advances. From the purely biological point of view it is unfortunate that the destructive side of technique has advanced so very much more rapidly than the creative side. (AAI 24)

PELAGIANISM

Pelagius was a Welshman, whose real name was Morgan, which means "man of the sea," as "Pelagius" does in Greek. He was a cultivated and agreeable ecclesiastic, less fanatical than many of his contemporaries. He believed in free will, questioned the doctrine of original sin, and thought that, when men act virtuously, it is by virtue of their own moral effort. If they act rightly, and are orthodox, they go to heaven as a reward for their virtues ... These views, though they may now seem commonplace, caused, at the time, a great commotion, and were, through Saint Augustine's efforts, declared heretical. (HWP 364)

PERCEPTION

In our environment it frequently happens that events occur together in bundles—such bundles as distinguish a cat from another kind of object. Any one of our senses may be affected by a stimulus arising from some characteristic of the bundle in question. Let us suppose the stimulus to be visual. Then physics allows us to infer that light of certain frequencies is proceeding from the object to our eyes.

Induction allows us to infer that this pattern of light, which, we will suppose, looks like a cat, probably proceeds from a region in which the other properties of cats are also present. Up to a point, we can test this hypothesis by experiment: we can touch the cat, and pick it up by the tail to see if it mews. Usually the experiment succeeds; when it does not, its failure is easily accounted for without modifying the laws of physics. (It is in this respect that physics is superior to ignorant common sense.) But all this elaborate work of induction, in so far as it belongs to common sense rather than science, is performed spontaneously by habit, which transforms the mere sensation into a perceptive experience. Broadly speaking, a perceptive experience is a dogmatic belief in what physics and induction show to be probable; it is wrong in its dogmatism, but *usually* right in its content. (IMT 152)

When a mental occurrence can be regarded as an appearance of an object external to the brain, however irregular, or even as a confused appearance of several such objects, then we may regard it as having for its stimulus the object or objects in question, or their appearances at the sense-organ concerned. When, on the other hand, a mental occurrence has not sufficient connection with objects external to the brain to be regarded as an appearance of such objects, then its physical causation (if any) will have to be sought in the brain. In the former case it can be called a perception; in the latter it cannot be so called. But the distinction is one of degree, not of kind. Until this is realized, no satisfactory theory of perception, sensation, or imagination is possible. (AM 136)

PERCEPTS AND PHYSICS

The gulf between percepts and physics is not a gulf as regards intrinsic quality, for we know nothing of the intrinsic quality of the physical world, and therefore do not know whether it is, or is not, very different from that of percepts. The gulf is as to what we know about the two realms. We know the quality of percepts, but we do not know their laws so well as we could wish. We know the laws of the physical world, in so far as these are mathematical, pretty well, but we know nothing else about it. If there is any intellectual difficulty in supposing that the physical world is intrinsically quite unlike that of percepts, this is a reason for supposing that there is not this complete unlikeness. And there is a certain ground for such a view, in the fact that percepts are part of the physical world, and are the only part that we can know without the help of rather elaborate and difficult inferences. (AOM 264)

PERFECTION

I do not imagine that mankind can be made perfect; whatever may be done, some defects will survive, but a great many of the defects from which adults suffer are due to preventable mistakes in their education, and the most important of these mistakes is the inculcation of fear. (EDTF 219)

PERSPECTIVE, INDIVIDUAL

For those to whom dogmatic religion can no longer bring comfort, there is need of some substitute, if life is not to become dusty and harsh and filled with trivial self-assertion. The world at present is full of angry self-centered groups, each incapable of viewing human life as a whole, each willing to destroy civilization rather than yield an inch. To this narrowness no amount of technical instruction will provide an antidote. The antidote, in so far as it is matter of individual psychology, is to be found in history, biology, astronomy, and all those studies which, without destroying self-respect, enable the individual to see himself in his proper perspective. (IPI 52)

PERSPECTIVES

The system consisting of all views of the universe perceived and unperceived, I shall call the system of "perspectives"; I shall confine the expression "private worlds" to such views of the universe as are actually perceived. Thus a "private world" is a perceived "perspective"; but there may be any number of unperceived perspectives. (KEW 93)

PESSIMISM

From a scientific point of view, optimism and pessimism are alike objectionable: optimism assumes, or attempts to prove, that the universe exists to please us, and pessimism that it exists to displease us. Scientifically, there is no evidence that it is concerned with us either one way or the other. The belief in either pessimism or optimism is a matter of temperament, not of reason. (HWP 759)

PHENOMENALISM

Intermediate between solipsism and the ordinary scientific view, there is a half-way house called "phenomenalism." This admits events other than those which I experience, but holds that all of them are percepts or other mental events. Practically, it means, when advocated by scientific men, that they will accept the testimony of other observers as to what they have actually experienced, but that they will not infer thence anything which no observer has experienced. It may be said, in justification of this position, that, while it employs analogy and induction, it refrains from assuming causality. But it may be doubted whether it can really abstain from causality. (AOM 399)

PHILO

The philosopher Philo, who was a contemporary of Christ, is the best illustration of Greek influence on the Jews in the sphere of thought. While orthodox in religion, Philo is, in philosophy, primarily a Platonist; other important influences are those of the Stoics and Neo-pythagoreans. While his influence among the Jews ceased after the fall of Jerusalem, the Christian Fathers found that he had shown the way to reconcile Greek philosophy with acceptance of the Hebrew Scriptures. (HWP 322)

PHILOSOPHER, STUDYING A

In studying a philosopher, the right attitude is neither reverence nor contempt, but first a kind of hypothetical sympathy, until it is possible to know what it feels like to believe in his theories, and only a revival of the critical attitude, which should resemble, as far as possible, the state of mind of a person abandoning opinions which he has hitherto held. (HWP 39)

PHILOSOPHERS

Most philosophers are extraordinarily dry and very dull; Descartes is neither dry nor dull, and that is very largely because he doesn't confine himself to strict logic, but puts in picturesque material of a biographical sort. (DDM 93)

PHILOSOPHERS, CHARACTERIZING

In attempting to characterize philosophers, no uniform method should be adopted. The method, in each case, should be such as to exhibit what the philosopher himself thinks important, and what, in the opinion of the critic, makes him worthy of study. (POS 453)

PHILOSOPHIC SPIRIT

A man imbued with the philosophic spirit, whether a professional philosopher or not, will wish his beliefs to be as true as he can make them, and will, in equal measure, love to know, and hate to be in error. This principle has a wider scope than may be apparent at first sight. (UE 30)

PHILOSOPHY

My purpose is to exhibit philosophy as an integral part of social and political life; not as the isolated speculations of remarkable individuals, but as both an effect and a cause of the character of the various communities in which different systems flourished. (HWP ix)

Philosophy, as I shall understand the word, is something intermediate between theology and science. Like theology, it consists of speculations on matters as to which definite knowledge has, so far, been unascertainable; but like science, it appeals to human reason rather than to authority, whether that of tradition or that of revelation. All *definite* knowledge—so I should contend—belongs to science; all *dogma* as to what surpasses definite knowledge belongs to theology. But between theology and science there is a No Man's Land, exposed to attack from both sides; this No Man's Land is philosophy. (HWP xiii)

Philosophy, as opposed to science, springs from a kind of self-assertion: a belief that our purposes have an important relation to the purpose of the universe, and that, in the long run, the course of events is bound to be, on the whole, such as we should wish. Science abandoned this kind of optimism, but is being led towards another: that we, by our intelligence, can make the world such as to satisfy a large proportion of our desires. This is a practical, as opposed to a metaphysical, optimism. I hope it will not seem to future generations as foolish as that of Dr. Pangloss. (UE 56-7)

Philosophy should be comprehensive, and should be bold in suggesting hypotheses as to the universe which science is not yet in a position to confirm or confute. But these should always be presented *as* hypotheses, not (as is too often done) as immutable certainties like the dogmas of religion. Although, moreover, comprehensive construction is part of the business of philosophy, I do not believe it is the most important part. The most important part, to my mind, consists in criticizing and clarifying notions which are apt to be regarded as fundamental and accepted uncritically. (LA 379)

The value of philosophy is, in fact, to be sought largely in its very uncertainty. The man who has no tincture of philosophy goes through life imprisoned in the prejudices derived from common sense, from the habitual beliefs of his age or his nation and from convictions which have grown up in his mind without the co-operation or consent of his deliberate reason. To such a man the world tends to become definite, finite, obvious; common objects rouse no questions, and unfamiliar possibilities are contemptuously rejected. As soon as we begin to philosophise, on the contrary, we find, as we saw in our opening chapters, that even the most everyday things lead to problems to which only very incomplete answers can be given. (PP 242-3)

PHILOSOPHY, FUNCTION OF

Apart from the attempt to understand the world, philosophy has other functions to fulfill. It can enlarge the imagination by the construction of a cosmic epic, or it can suggest a way of life less wayward and accidental than that of the unreflective. A philosopher who attempts either of these tasks must be judged by a standard of values, aesthetic or ethical, rather than by intellectual correctness. (POS 453)

Leaving aside, for the moment, all questions that have to

do with ethics or with values, there are a number of purely theoretical questions, of perennial and passionate interest, which science is unable to answer, at any rate at present. Do we survive death in any sense, and if so, do we survive for a time or forever? Can mind dominate matter, or does matter completely dominate mind, or has each, perhaps, a certain limited independence? Has the universe a purpose? Or is it driven by blind necessity? Or is it a mere chaos and jumble, in which the natural laws that we think we find are only a fantasy generated by our love of order? If there is a cosmic scheme, has life more importance in it than astronomy would lead us to suppose, or is our emphasis upon life mere parochialism and self-importance? I do not know the answer to these questions, and I do not believe that anybody else does, but I think human life would be impoverished if they were forgotten, or if definite answers were accepted without adequate evidence. To keep alive the interest in such questions, and to scrutinize suggested answers, is one of the functions of philosophy. (UE 25-6)

PHILOSOPHY, INDUSTRIAL

The dominating belief of what may be called the industrial philosophy is that man is master of his fate, and need not submit tamely to the evils hitherto inflicted upon him by the niggardliness of inanimate nature or the follies of human nature. Man was in the past dependent upon the weather, which was beyond his control. This is still the case with peasants, who are usually pious, and still more so with fishermen, who are still more pious. It may be laid down broadly that the intensity of religious belief among seafaring folk is inversely proportional to the size of their vessel. (S 67)

PHILOSOPHY, PLACE OF

But there is a second problem, less precise, and by some mistakenly regarded as unimportant—I mean the problem of how best to utilize our command over the forces of nature. This includes such burning issues as democracy versus dictatorship, capitalism versus socialism, international government versus international anarchy, free speculation versus authoritarian dogma. On such issues the laboratory can give no decisive guidance. The kind of knowledge that gives most help in solving such problems is a wide survey of human life, in the past as well as in the present, and an appreciation of the sources of misery or contentment as they appear in history. (UE 21)

PHILOSOPHY, PROFESSIONAL

"Philosophy" means "love of wisdom," and philosophy in this sense is what men must acquire if the new powers invented by technicians, and handed over by them to be wielded by ordinary men and women, are not to plunge mankind into an appalling cataclysm. But the philosophy that should be a part of general education is not the same thing as the philosophy of specialists. Not only in philosophy, but in all branches of academic study, there is a distinction between what has cultural value and what is only of professional interest. (UE 22)

PHILOSOPHY, SCIENTIFIC

A scientific philosophy such as I wish to recommend will be piecemeal and tentative like other sciences; above all, it will be able to invent hypotheses which, even if they are not wholly true, will yet remain fruitful after the necessary corrections have been made. This possibility of successive approximations to the truth is more than anything else, the source of the triumphs of science, and to transfer this possibility to philosophy is to ensure a progress in method whose importance it would be almost impossible to exaggerate. (ML 113)

PHILOSOPHY, STUDY OF

And since the philosophies of the past belong to one or other of a few great types—types which in our own day are perpetually recurring—we may learn, from examining the greatest representative of any type, what are the grounds for such a philosophy. (PL xii)

PHILOSOPHY, VALUE OF

It can give a habit of exact and careful thought, not only in mathematics and science, but in questions of large practical import. It can give an impersonal breadth and scope to the conception of the ends of life. It can give to the individual a just measure of himself in relation to society, of man in the present to man in the past and in the future, and of the whole history of man in relation to the astronomical cosmos. By enlarging the objects of his thoughts it supplies an antidote to the anxieties and anguish of the present, and makes possible the nearest approach to serenity that is available to a sensitive mind in our tortured and uncertain world. (UE 32-3)

PHYSICAL OBJECT

According to the view that I am suggesting, a physical object or piece of matter is the collection of all those correlated particulars which would be regarded by common sense as its effects or appearances in different places. On the other hand, all the happenings in a given place represent what common sense would regard as the appearances of a number of different objects as viewed from that place. All the happenings in one place may be regarded as the view of the world from that place. I shall call the view of the world from a given place a "perspective." (AM 101)

PHYSICS

Physics must be interpreted in a way which tends toward idealism, and perception in a way which tends toward materialism. I believe that matter is less material, and mind less mental, than is commonly supposed, and that, when this is realized, the difficulties raised by Berkeley largely disappear. (AOM 7)

PHYSICS, MODERN

The extreme abstractness of modern physics makes it difficult to understand, but gives to those who can understand it a grasp of the world as a whole, a sense of its structure and mechanism, which no less abstract apparatus could possibly supply. The power of using abstractions is the essence of intellect, and with every increase in abstraction triumphs of science are enhanced. (SO 84)

PLEASURE, CALCULUS OF

The intellectual conviction that pleasure is the sole good, together with a temperamental incapacity for experiencing it, was characteristic of Utilitarians. From the point of view of the calculus of pleasures and pains, their emotional poverty was advantageous: they tended to think that pleasure could be measured by the bank-account, and pain by fines or terms of imprisonment. Unselfish and stoical devotion to the doctrine that every man seeks only his own pleasure is a curious psychological paradox. (FO 98)

PLEBISCITES

Any constitutional change in any country therefore should in future be sanctioned by a plebiscite, not imposed by an armed minority; and any regional minority should have the power of presenting its grievances to an international authority, which should be empowered to conduct a plebiscite in the region concerned to determine whether or not it should be granted local autonomy. (ISIP 231)

PLOTINUS

Plotinus, however, is not *only* historically important. He represents, better than any other philosopher, an important type of theory. A philosophical system may be judged important for various different kinds of reasons. The first and most obvious is that we think it may be true. Not many students of philosophy at the present time would feel this about Plotinus; Dean Inge is, in this respect, a rare exception. But truth is not the only merit that a metaphysic can possess. It may have beauty, and this is certainly to be found in Plotinus. (HWP 285)

PLURALISM

Pluralism is the view of science and common sense, and is therefore to be accepted, if the arguments against it are not conclusive. For my part, I have no doubt whatever that it is the true view, and that monism is derived from a faulty logic inspired by mysticism. This logic dominates the philosophy of Hegel and his followers; it is also the essential basis of Bergson's system, although it is seldom mentioned in his writings. When it is rejected, ambitious metaphysical systems such as those of the past are seen to be impossible. (OP 253)

POSSIBILITY, SYNTACTIC

There is one sense of the word "possibility" which is connected with our present problem. We may say that whatever is asserted by a significant sentence has a certain kind of possibility. I will define this as "syntactic" possibility. It is perhaps narrower than logical possibility, but certainly wider than physical possibility. (IMT 214)

POSTULATES

Science cannot dispense wholly with postulates, but as it advances their number decreases. I mean by a postulate something not very different from a working hypothesis, except that it is more general: it is something which we assume without sufficient evidence, in the hope that, by its help, we shall be able to construct a theory which the facts will confirm. It is by no means essential to science to assume that its postulates are true always or necessarily; it is enough if they are often true. (AOM 167)

POWER

The mere possession of power tends to produce a love of power, which is a very dangerous motive, because the only sure proof of power consists in preventing others from doing what they wish to do. The essential theory of democracy is the diffusion of power among the whole people, so that the evils produced by one man's possession of great power shall be obviated. But the diffusion of power through democracy is only effective when the voters take an interest in the question involved. (PI 85-6)

Power may be defined as ability to cause people to act as we wish, when they would have acted otherwise but for the effects of our desires; it includes also ability to prevent people from acting against our wishes, which is sometimes the utmost that we aim at achieving—for instance, in the case of a murderer who is executed. (PIC 190)

But unless the power of officials can be kept within bounds, socialism will mean little more than the substitution of one set of masters for another: all the former powers of the capitalist will be inherited by the official. (ISOS 37)

POWER, PROPER USE OF

There must be power, either that of governments, or that of anarchic adventurers. There must even be naked power, so long as there are rebels against governments, or even ordinary criminals. But if human life is to be, for the mass of mankind, anything better than a dull misery punctuated with moments of sharp horror, there must be as little naked power as possible. The exercise of power, if it is to be something better than the infliction of wanton torture, must be hedged round by safeguards of law and custom, permitted only after due deliberation, and entrusted to men who are closely supervised in the interests of those who are subjected to them. I do not pretend that this is easy. (P 104)

POWER, UNRESTRICTED

Soviet imperialism, Soviet bad faith, Soviet refusal to prevent an atomic armament race—all these things are bad, but they are not so new as the internal evils. In Russia, as in a vast human laboratory, the student can see the result of allowing the power impulse unrestricted scope in a modern monolithic state. It is a terrible spectacle, and it all springs from mistakes in Lenin's thinking. (CTR 37)

POWER, USE OF

The ultimate aim of those who have power (and we all have some) should be to promote social co-operation, not in one group as against another, but in the whole human race. The chief obstacle to this end at present is the existence of feelings of unfriendliness and desire for superiority. Such feelings can be diminished either directly by religion and morality, or indirectly by removing the political and economic circumstances which at present stimulate them—notably the competition for power between States and the connected competition for wealth between large national industries. Both methods are needed: they are not alternatives, but supplement each other. (P 271)

PRAGMATISM

Pragmatism muddles up the practical and philosophical in a way I don't like; I am an admirer of certain passions, but I don't admire a philosophy made up, like pragmatism, of unduly practical theory and unduly theoretical practice. (TWW 17)

Although pragmatism may not contain ultimate philosophical truth, it has certain important merits. First, it realizes that the truth that *we* can attain to is merely human truth, fallible and changeable like everything human. What lies outside the cycle of human occurrences is not truth, but fact (of certain kinds). Truth is a property of beliefs, and beliefs are psychical events. Moreover their relation to facts does not have the schematic simplicity which logic assumes; to have pointed this out is a second merit in pragmatism. (SE 63)

PROBABILITY

The theory of probability is in a very unsatisfactory state, both logically and mathematically; and I do not believe that there is any alchemy by which it can produce regularity in large numbers out of pure caprice in each single case. If the penny really chose by caprice whether to fall heads or tails, have we any reason to say that it would choose one about as often as the other? Might not caprice lead just as well always to the same choice? This is no more than a suggestion, since the subject is too obscure for dogmatic statements. (RAS 168)

For this reason the inductive principle cannot be proved or disproved by experience. We might prove validly that such and such a conclusion was enormously probable, and yet it might not happen. We might prove invalidly that it was probable, and yet it might happen. What happens affects the probability of proposition, since it is relevant evidence; but it never alters the probability relative to the previously available evidence. The whole subject of probability, therefore, on Mr. Keynes's theory, is strictly *a priori* and independent of experience. (OP 274-5)

PROPAGANDA

We are beginning to understand the art of manufacturing opinions wholesale as we manufacture pins. The technique is not yet quite perfect, but it may be confidently hoped that within another hundred years almost every citizen of a state will have, on almost every subject, the opinions which the Government of that state wishes him to have. (SSI 18)

Propaganda is only successful when it is in harmony with something in the patient: his desire for an immortal soul, for health, for the greatness of his nation, or what not. Where there is no such fundamental reason for acquiescence, the assertions of authority are viewed with cynical skepticism. (P 141)

The art of propaganda, as practised by modern politicians and Governments, is derived from the art of advertisement. The science of psychology owes a great deal to advertisers. In former days most psychologists would probably have thought that a man could not convince many people of the excellence of his own wares by merely stating emphatically that they were excellent. Experience shows, however, that they were mistaken in this. (FT 36-7)

Propaganda may be defined as any attempt, by means of persuasion, to enlist human beings in the service of one party to any dispute. It is thus distinguished from persecution by its method, which is one that eschews force, and from instruction by its motive, which is not the dissemination of knowledge, but the generating of some kind of party feeling. (ESO 207)

PROPERTY

The essence of private property is legal possession, secured to some person or group within the state, together with the rights built upon that possession. It is not essential that the possessor should be an individual. (PIC 43)

PROPHECIES

I have spoken of a two-fold movement in past history, but I do not consider that there is anything either certain or inevitable about such laws of historical development as we can discover. New knowledge may make the course of events completely different from what it would otherwise have been; this was, for instance, a result of the discovery of America. New institutions also may have effects that could not have been foreseen: I do not see how any Roman at the time of Julius Caesar could have predicted anything at all like the Catholic Church. And no one in the nineteenth century, not even Marx, foresaw the Soviet Union. For such reasons, all prophecies as to the future of mankind should be treated only as hypotheses which may deserve consideration. (AAI 43)

PROPOSITION

We mean by a "proposition" primarily a form of words which expresses what is either true or false. I say "primarily," because I do not wish to exclude other than verbal symbols, or even mere thoughts if they have a symbolic character. But I think the word "proposition" should be limited to what may, in some sense, be called "symbols," and further to such symbols as give expression to truth and falsehood. (IMP 155)

A proposition is something which may be said in any language: "Socrates is mortal" and "Socrate est mortel" express the same proposition. In a given language it may be said in various ways: the difference between "Caesar was killed on the Ides of March" and "it was on the Ides of March that Caesar was killed" is merely rhetorical. It is thus possible for two forms of words to "have the same meaning." We may, at least for the moment, define a "proposition" as "all the sentences which have the same meaning as some given sentence." (IMT 10)

A form of words which must be either true or false, I shall call a *proposition*. (KEW 55)

PROPOSITIONAL ATTITUDES

There is another very important class of words that must be at least provisionally excluded, namely such words as "believe," "desire," "doubt," all of which, when they occur in a sentence, must be followed by a subordinate sentence telling what it is that is believed or desired or doubted. Such words, so far as I have been able to discover, are always psychological, and involve what I call "propositional attitudes." For the present, I will merely point out that they differ from such words as "or" in an important respect, namely that they are necessary for the description of observable phenomena. (IMT 79)

PROPOSITIONAL FUNCTION

"A propositional function" is an expression containing one or more undetermined constituents x, y, . . . , and such that, if we settle what these are to be, the result is a proposition. Thus "x is a man" is a propositional function, because, if you decide on a value for x, the result is a proposition—a true proposition if you define that x is to be Socrates or Plato, a false proposition if x is to be Cerberus or Pegasus. The values for which it is true constitute the class of men. Every propositional function determines a class, namely the class of values of the variable for which it is true. (IMT 326)

PROPOSITIONS, NEGATIVE

Let us consider, in like manner, negative propositions which seem to have an immediate relation to experience. Suppose you are told "there is butter in the larder, but no cheese." Although they seem equally based upon sensible experience in the larder, the two statements "there is butter" and "there is not cheese" are really on a very different level. There was a definite occurrence which was seeing butter, and which might have put the word "butter" into your mind even if you had not been thinking of butter. (IMT 89)

PROSTITUTION

Prostitution as it exists at present is obviously an undesirable kind of life. The risk of disease in itself renders prostitution a dangerous trade, like working in white lead, but apart from that the life is a demoralizing one. It is idle; and tends to excessive drinking. It has the grave drawback that the prostitute is generally despised, and is probably thought ill of even by her clients. It is a life against instinct—quite as much against instinct as the life of a nun. For all these reasons prostitution, as it exists in Christian countries, is an extraordinarily undesirable career. (MM 150)

PROTAGORAS

He is chiefly noted for his doctrine that "Man is the measure of all things, of things that are that they are, and of things that are not that they are not." This is interpreted as meaning that *each* man is the measure of all things, and that, when men differ, there is no objective truth in virtue of which one is right and the other wrong. The doctrine is essentially sceptical, and is presumably based on the "deceitfulness" of the senses. (HWP 77)

PROTECTION

It was the German economist List who first (in 1841) provided a theoretical defence of protectionism. This was the famous "infant industries" argument. Take, say, steel. It may be that a country is well suited by nature to the development of a great steel industry, but that, owing to foreign competition, the initial expenses are prohibitive, unless government assistance is obtainable. This situation existed in Germany when List wrote and for some time after that. But experience has shown that protection, once granted, cannot be withdrawn even when the infant has grown into a giant. (FO 142)

PSYCHO-ANALYSIS

Psycho-analysis, though no doubt it has its exaggerations, and even perhaps absurdities, has taught us a great deal that is true and valuable. It is an old saying that even if you expel nature with a pitchfork it will still come back, but psycho-analysis has supplied the commentary to this text. We now know that a life which goes excessively against natural impulse is one which is likely to involve effects of strain that may be quite as bad as indulgence in forbidden impulses would have been. People who live a life which is unnatural beyond a point are likely to be filled with envy, malice and uncharitableness. (AAI 20-1)

Whatever may be thought of psycho-analysis, there is one point in which it is unquestionably in the right, and that is in the enormous stress which it lays upon the emotional life. Given the right emotional development, both character and intelligence ought to develop spontaneously. It is, therefore, to the emotions above all that the scientific educator should direct his attention. (SAE 88)

For our purposes, the essential discovery of psycho-analysis is this: that an impulse which is prevented, by behaviourist methods, from finding overt expression in action, does not necessarily die, but is driven underground, and finds some new outlet which has not been inhibited by training. Often the new outlet will be more harmful than the one that has been prevented, and in any case the deflection involves emotional disturbance and unprofitable expenditure of energy. (ESO 55)

Psycho-analysis, as every one knows, is primarily a method of understanding hysteria and certain forms of insanity; but it has been found that there is much in the lives of ordinary men and women which bears a humiliating resemblance to the delusions of the insane. The connection of dreams, irrational beliefs and foolish actions with unconscious wishes has been brought to light, though with some exaggeration, by Freud and Jung and their followers. As regards the nature of these unconscious wishes it seems to me—though as a layman I speak with diffidence—that many psycho-analysts are unduly narrow; no doubt the wishes they emphasize exist, but others, e.g. for honour and power, are equally operative and equally liable to concealment. (AM 32-3)

PSYCHOLOGY AND PHYSICS

It follows that if physics is an empirical science, whose statements can be confirmed or confuted by observation, then physics must be supplemented by laws connecting stimulus and sensation. Now such laws belong to psychology. Therefore what is empirically verifiable is not pure physics in isolation, but physics plus a department of psychology. Psychology, accordingly, is an essential ingredient in every part of empirical science. (HK 49)

PSYCHOLOGY, CHILD

If you could take children more naturally and spontaneously and not bother so much about child psychology, it would be very much better I think. (CAW 217)

PSYCHOTHERAPY

Such a desire is generally, in morbid cases, of a sort which the patient would consider wicked; if he had to admit that he had the desire, he would loathe himself. Yet it is so strong that it must force an outlet for itself; hence it becomes necessary to entertain whole systems of false beliefs in order to hide the nature of what is desired. The resulting delusions in very many cases disappear if the hysteric or lunatic can be made to face the facts about himself. The consequence of this is that the treatment of many forms of insanity has grown more psychological and less physiological than it used to be. (AM 33-4)

PUBLIC DEFENDER

If law-abiding citizens are to be protected against unjust persecution by the police, there must be two police forces and two Scotland Yards, one designed, as at present, to prove guilt, the other to prove innocence. . . . (P 283-4)

PUBLIC OPINION, INTERNATIONAL

No mechanism, however perfect, will work unless it is supported by a strong public opinion. The establishment of an international government will not be successful unless most of the civilized nations have become persuaded that unrestricted national sovereignty involves disaster. (WWP 84)

PUBLIC OWNERSHIP, CONTROL OF

While, therefore, public ownership and control of all large-scale industry and finance is a *necessary* condition for the training of power, it is far from being a *sufficient* condition. It needs to be supplemented by a democracy more thoroughgoing, more carefully safeguarded against official tyranny, and with more deliberate provision for freedom of propaganda, than any purely political democracy that ever existed. (P 290)

PUNCTUALITY

Another rather humble virtue which is not likely to be produced by a wholly free education is punctuality. Punctuality is a quality the need of which is bound up with social co-operation. It has nothing to do with the relation of the soul to God, or with mystic insight, or with any of the matters with which the more elevated and spiritual moralists are concerned. One would be surprised to find a saint getting drunk, but one would not be surprised to find him late for an engagement. And yet in the ordinary business of life punctuality is absolutely necessary. (ESO 34-5)

Q

QUANTITATIVE TEST IN EDUCATION

One of the characteristics of the scientific method is that it is quantitative and aims at discovering the just balance of the different ingredients required to produce a good result, whereas pre-scientific methods consider some things good and some bad without regard to quantity. Take, for example, the question of the quantity of adult attention that is best for a child. In old days most children got less of this than they should have had; nowadays, most children of the well-to-do get more. (SAE 94)

R

RACE

About race, if politics were not involved, it would be enough to say that nothing politically important is known. It may be taken as probable that there are genetic mental differences between races; but it is certain that we do not yet know what these differences are. In an adult man, the effects of environment mask those of heredity. (IPI 113)

There is a special absurdity in applying racial theories to the various populations of Europe. There is not in Europe any such thing as a pure race. Russians have an admixture of Tartar blood, Germans are largely Slavonic, France is a mixture of Celts, Germans, and people of Mediterranean race, Italy the same with the addition of the descendants of slaves imported by the Romans. The English are perhaps the most mixed of all. There is no evidence that there is any advantage in belonging to a pure race. The purest races now in existence are the Pygmies, the Hottentots, and the Australian aborigines; the Tasmanians, who were probably even purer, are extinct. (UE 89-90)

RADICALISM

Radicalism, unlike Liberalism, was a doctrine inspired by economic considerations, especially such as were suggested by nascent industrialism. Radicals were even more individualistic than Liberals, since they took no interest in nations. As individuals they may have been liable to patriotism, but as theorists they were cosmopolitan. They believed in free trade, free competition, free individual initiative within the limits of the criminal law. They did not object to the power of property, so long as the property had been acquired by personal effort, not by privilege or inheritance (FO 448)

RADICALS, THE PHILOSOPHICAL

The Philosophical Radicals, as a school, had certain important merits which, in our day, are apt to be overlooked. They applied to all existing institutions the test of utility, and accepted nothing on the mere ground of historical prescription. By this test, they found no justification for monarchy, aristocracy, religion, war, or empire. Liberals had a rhetorical and sentimental objection to some of these, but the objections of Philosophical Radicals were argumentative, calm and apparently derived from the inexorable voice of Reason. (FO 449)

RATIONALISM

Rationalism and anti-rationalism have existed side by side since the beginning of Greek civilization, and each, when it had seemed likely to become completely dominant, has always led, by reaction, to a new outburst of its opposite. (IPI 102)

RATIONALISTS

... the rationalists—who are represented by the Continental philosophers of the seventeenth century, especially Descartes and Leibniz—maintained that, in addition to what we know by experience, there are certain "innate ideas" and "innate principles," which we know independently of experience. (PP 114-5)

RATIONALITY

Rationality in practice may be defined as the habit of remembering all our relevant desires, and not only the one which happens at the moment to be strongest. Like rationality in opinion, it is a matter of degree. Complete rationality is no doubt an unattainable ideal, but so long as we continue to classify some men as lunatics it is clear that we think some men more rational than others. I believe that all solid progress in the world consists of an increase in rationality, both practical and theoretical. (SE 54)

RATIONALIZING

Freudians have accustomed us to "rationalizing", i.e., the process of inventing what seem to ourselves rational grounds for a decision or opinion that is in fact quite irrational. But there is, especially in English speaking countries, a converse process which may be called "irrationalizing." A shrewd man will sum up, more or less subconsciously, the pros and cons of a question from a selfish point of view. (Unselfish considerations seldom weigh subconsciously except where one's children are concerned.) Having come to a sound egoistic decision by the help of the unconscious, a man proceeds to invent, or adopt from others, a set of high-sounding phrases showing how he is pursuing the public good at immense personal sacrifice. (SE 20-1)

REACTIONS, SUSPENDED

Sentences are needed to distinguish between these various uses of words. They are needed also—and this is perhaps their main use—to express what may be called "suspended reactions." Suppose you intend to take a railway journey tomorrow, and you look up your train today; you do not propose, at the moment, to take any further action on the knowledge you have acquired, but when the time comes you will behave in the appropriate manner. Knowledge, in the sense in which it does not merely register present sensible impressions, consists essentially of preparations for such delayed reactions. Such preparations may in all cases be called "beliefs," but they are only to be called "knowledge" when they prompt *successful* reactions, or at any rate show themselves related to the facts with which they are concerned in some way which distinguishes them from preparations that would be called "errors." (HK 94)

REAL

The supposed "real" table underlying its appearances is, in any case, not itself perceived, but inferred, and the question whether such-and-such a particular is an "aspect" of this table is only to be settled by the connection of the particular in question with the one or more particulars by which the table is "defined." That is to say, even if we assume a "real" table, the particulars which are its aspects have to be collected together by their relations to each other, not to it, since it is merely inferred from them. (AM 98)

REALISM

I think Pierce was right in regarding the realist-nominalist controversy as one which is still undecided, and which is as important as at any former time. (FPF xv)

The view which I should wish to advocate is that objects of perception do not persist unchanged at times when they are not perceived, although probably objects more or less resembling them do exist at such times, that objects of perception are part, and the only empirically knowable part, of the actual subject-matter of physics, and are themselves properly to be called physical; that purely physical laws exist determining the character and duration of objects of perception without any reference to the fact that they are perceived; and that in the establishment of such laws the propositions of physics do not presuppose any propositions of psychology or even the existence of mind. I do not know whether realists would recognize such a view as realism. All that I should claim for it is, that it avoids difficulties which seem to me to beset both realism and idealism as hitherto advocated, and that it avoids the appeal which they have made to ideas which logical analysis shows to be ambiguous. (ML 123)

REALISM, SCHOLASTIC

Scholastic realism was a metaphysical theory, but every metaphysical theory has a technical counterpart. I had been a realist in the scholastic or Platonic sense; I had thought that cardinal integers, for instance, have a timeless being. When integers were reduced to classes of classes, this being was transferred to classes. Meinong, whose work interested me, applied the argument of realism to descriptive phrases. Everyone agrees that "the golden mountain does not exist" is a true proposition. But it has, apparently, a subject, "the golden mountain," and if this subject did not designate some object, the proposition would seem to be meaningless. Meinong inferred that there is a golden mountain which is golden and a mountain, but does not exist. He even thought that the existent golden mountain is existent, but does not exist. This did not satisfy me, and the desire to avoid Meinong's unduly populous realm of being led me to the theory of descriptions. What was of importance in this theory was the discovery that, in analysing a significant sentence, one must not assume that each separate word or phrase has significance on its own account. "The golden mountain" can be part of a significant sentence, but is not significant in isolation. It soon appeared that class-symbols could be treated like descriptions . . . (MMD 13-4)

REALITY

The question we have therefore to consider is the question as to what can be meant by assigning "reality" to some but not all of the entities that make up the world. Two elements, I think, make up what is felt rather than thought when the word "reality" is used in this sense. A thing is real if it persists at times when it is not perceived; or again, a thing is real when it is correlated with other things in a way which experience has led us to expect. It will be seen that reality in either of these senses is by no means necessary to a thing, and that in fact there might be a whole world in which nothing was real in either of these senses. It might turn out that the objects of perception failed of reality in one or both of these respects, without its being in any way deducible that they are not parts of the external world with which physics deals. (ML 121-2)

REASON

I do not mean by "reason" any faculty of determining the ends of life. The ends which a man will pursue are determined by his desires; but he may pursue them wisely or unwisely. We may assume that the kaiser hoped to increase his power by the war, and that the czar hoped to avert revolution; neither of them showed wisdom in the choice of means to these ends. When I speak of "reason," I mean merely the endeavor to find out the truth about any matter with which we are concerned, as opposed to the endeavor to prove to ourselves that what we desire is true. (PIC 225)

Reason is a harmonising, controlling force rather than a creative one. Even in the most purely logical realm, it is insight that first arrives at what is new. (ML 13)

I think that what we mean in practice by reason can be defined by three characteristics. In the first place, it relies upon persuasion rather than force; in the second place, it seeks to persuade by means of arguments, which the man who uses them believes to be completely valid; and in the third place, in forming opinions, it uses observation and induction as much as possible and intuition as little as possible. (IPI 99-100)

REASON, PRINCIPLE OF SUFFICIENT

This brings me to the principle of sufficient reason. This principle is usually supposed to be, by itself, adequate to the deduction of what actually exists. To this supposition, it must be confessed, Leibniz's words often lend colour. But we shall find that there are really two principles included under the same name, the one general, and applying to all possible worlds, the other special, and applying only to the actual world. Both differ from the law of contradiction, by the fact that they apply specially—the former, however, not exclusively—to existents, possible or actual. (PL 30)

REBELLION

I do not mean to be understood as an advocate of rebellion. Rebellion in itself is no better than acquiescence in itself, since it is equally determined by relation to what is outside ourselves rather than by a purely personal judgment of value. Whether rebellion is to be praised or deprecated depends upon that against which a person rebels, but there should be the possibility of rebellion on occasion, and not only a blind acquiescence produced by a rigid education in conformity. And what is perhaps more important than either rebellion or acquiescence, there should be the capacity to strike out a wholly new line, as was done by Pythagoras when he invented the study of geometry. (ESO 14)

Without rebellion, mankind would stagnate, and injustice would be irremediable. The man who refuses to obey authority has, therefore, in certain circumstances, a legitimate function, provided his disobedience has motives which are social rather than personal. But the matter is one as to which, by its very nature, it is impossible to lay down rules. (P 252)

REFLEX, LAW OF CONDITIONED AND UNCONDITIONED

The fundamental law in this subject is the law of conditioned reflexes; when the stimulus to an unconditioned reflex has been repeatedly accompanied, or immediately preceded, by some other stimulus, this other stimulus alone will, in time, equally produce the response which was originally called forth by the stimulus to the unconditioned reflex. (SO 49)

REFORM

The method of gradual reform has many merits as compared to the method of revolution, and I have no wish to preach revolution. (PI 74)

REFORM, PENAL

I do not wish, however, to embark upon the subject of Penal Reform. I merely wish to suggest that we should treat the criminal as we treat a man suffering from plague. Each is a public danger, each must have his liberty curtailed until he has ceased to be a danger. But the man suffering from plague is an object of sympathy and commiseration, whereas the criminal is an object of execration. (WIB 54)

REFORMATION

From the sixteenth century onward, the history of European thought is dominated by the Reformation. The Reformation was a complex many-sided movement, and owed its success to a variety of causes. In the main, it was a revolt of the northern nations against the renewed dominion of Rome. Religion was the force that had subdued the North, but religion in Italy had decayed: the papacy remained as an institution, and extracted a huge tribute from Germany and England, but these nations, which were still pious, could feel no reverence for the Borgias and Medicis, who professed to save souls from purgatory in return for cash which they squandered on luxury and immorality. National motives, economic motives, and moral motives all combined to strengthen the revolt against Rome. (HWP xix-xx)

REGION, MINIMAL

We will define a set of comprexent events as a "minimal region." We find that minimal regions form a four-dimensional manifold, and that, by a little logical manipulation, we can construct from them the manifold of space-time that physics requires. (LA 381)

RELATIVITY

A certain type of superior person is fond of asserting that "everything is relative." This is, of course, nonsense, because if *everything* were relative, there would be nothing for it to be relative to. However, without falling into metaphysical absurdities it is possible to maintain that everything in the physical world is relative to an observer. (ABCR 14)

Two events in distant places may appear simultaneous to one observer who has taken all due precautions to insure accuracy (and, in particular, has allowed for the velocity of light), while another equally careful observer may judge that the first event preceded the second, and still another may judge that the second preceded the first. This would happen if the three observers were all moving rapidly relatively to each other. (ABCR 43)

RELIGION

"Religion" is a word which has many meanings and a long history. In origin, it was concerned with certain rites, inherited from a remote past, performed originally for some reason long since forgotten, and associated from time to time with various myths to account for their supposed importance. Much of this lingers still. (PSR 223)

By a religion, I mean a set of beliefs held as dogmas, dominating the conduct of life, going beyond or contrary to evidence, and inculcated by methods which are emotional or authoritarian, not intellectual. By this definition, Bolshevism is a religion: that its dogmas go beyond or contrary to evidence, I shall try to prove in what follows. Those who accept Bolshevism become impervious to scientific evidence, and commit intellectual suicide. Even if all the doctrines of Bolshevism were true, this would still be the case, since no unbiased examination of them is tolerated. One who believes, as I do, that the free intellect is the chief engine of human progress, cannot but be fundamentally opposed to Bolshevism, as much as to the Church of Rome. (PTB 117-8)

RELIGION AND EVOLUTION

Religion, in our day, has accommodated itself to the doctrine of evolution, and has even derived new arguments from it. We are told that "through the ages one increasing purpose runs," and that evolution is the unfolding of an idea which has been in the mind of God throughout. It appears that during those ages which so troubled Hugh Miller, when animals were torturing each other with ferocious horns and agonizing stings, Omnipotence was quietly waiting for the ultimate emergence of man, with his still more exquisite powers of torture and his far more widely diffused cruelty. Why the Creator should have preferred to reach His goal by a process, instead of going straight to it, these modern theologians do not tell us. (RAS 81)

RELIGION, ELEMENTS OF

The three elements of religion, namely worship, acquiescence, and love, are intimately interconnected; each helps to produce the others, and all three together form a unity in which it is impossible to say which comes first, which last. All three can exist without dogma, in a form which is capable of dominating life and of giving infinity to action and thought and feeling; and life in the infinite, which is the combination of the three, contains all that is essential to religion, in spite of its absence of dogmatic beliefs. (ER 59)

RELIGION, ORGANIZED

The immense majority of ministers of religion support war whenever it occurs, though in peace time they are often pacifists; in supporting war, they give emphatic utterance to their conviction that God is on their side, and lend religious support to the persecution of men who think wholesale slaughter unwise. While slavery existed, religious arguments were found in support of it; now-a-days, similar arguments are found in support of capitalistic exploitation. Almost all traditional cruelties and injustices have been supported by organised religion until the moral sense of the lay community compelled a change of front. (ESO 107)

RELIGION, PSYCHOLOGY OF

It would seem, therefore, that the three human impulses embodied in religion are fear, conceit, and hatred. The purpose of religion, one may say, is to give an air of respectability to these passions provided they run in certain channels. It is because these passions make on the whole for human misery that religion is a force for evil, since it permits men to indulge these passions without restraint, where but for its sanction they might, at least to a certain degree, control them. (RUC 26)

RENAISSANCE

The main motive of the Renaissance was mental delight, the restoration of a certain richness and freedom in art and speculation which had been lost while ignorance and superstition kept the mind's eye in blinkers. (IPI 38)

The Renaissance was not a period of great achievement in philosophy, but it did certain things which were essential preliminaries to the greatness of the seventeenth century. In the first place, it broke down the rigid scholastic system, which had become an intellectual strait jacket. It revived the study of Plato, and thereby demanded at least so much independent thought as was required for choosing between him and Aristotle. In regard to both, it promoted a genuine and first-hand knowledge, free from the glosses of Neoplatonists and Arabic commentators. More important still, it encouraged the habit of regarding intellectual activity as a delightful social adventure, not a cloistered meditation aiming at the preservation of a predetermined orthodoxy. (HWP 500)

RENT, RICARDO'S THEORY OF

Ricardo's theory of rent is simple, and in suitable circumstances perfectly valid. In considering it, let us, to begin with, confine ourselves to agricultural land. Some land is more fertile, some less; at any given moment, there must be some land on the margin of cultivation, which is only just worth cultivating. That is to say, it just yields a return to the farmer's capital which is equal to what the same capital would yield if otherwise invested. If the landlord were to demand rent for this land, the farmer would no longer find it worth cultivating; such land, therefore, will yield no rent to the landlord. On more fertile land, on the contrary, a given amount of capital yields more than the usual rate of profit; therefore the farmer is willing to pay the landlord for the right to cultivate it. What he is willing to pay is the excess of the produce above what is yielded by the same amount of the worst land in cultivation. Thus the rent of an acre of land is the amount by which the value of the crop that can be raised on it exceeds the value of the crop that can be raised on an acre of the worst land in cultivation. (FO 103-4)

REPRESENTATIVE GOVERNMENT, DEMOCRATIC

I am a firm believer in democratic representative government as the best form for those who have the tolerance and self-restraint that is required to make it workable. But its advocates make a mistake if they suppose that it can be at once introduced into countries where the average citizen has hitherto lacked all training in the give-and-take that it requires. In a Balkan country, not so many years ago, a party which had been beaten by a narrow margin in a general election retrieved its fortunes by shooting a sufficient number of the representatives of the other side to give it a majority. People in the West thought this characteristic of the Balkans, forgetting that Cromwell and Robespierre had acted likewise. (UE 140)

REVERENCE

Those who realize the harm that can be done to others by any use of force against them, and the worthlessness of the goods that can be acquired by force, will be very full of respect for the liberty of others; they will not try to bind them or fetter them; they will be slow to judge and swift to sympathize; they will treat every human being with a kind of tenderness, because the principle of good in him is at once fragile and infinitely precious. They will not condemn those who are unlike themselves; they will know and feel that individuality brings differences and uniformity means death. They will wish each human being to be as much a living thing and as little a mechanical product as it is possible to be; they will cherish in each one just those things which the harsh usage of a ruthless world would destroy. In one word, all their dealings with others will be inspired by a deep impulse of *reverence*. (PI 12-3)

REVOLUTION

In my mind, I should not think any gain worth civil war or armed rebellion. I do not think any good comes of that and I think we must rely on persuasion and peaceful propaganda. Otherwise, we shall get nowhere. (TEP 11)

Apart from all arguments of detail, there are two broad objections to violent revolution in a democratic community. The first is that, when once the principle of respecting majorities as expressed at the ballot-box is abandoned, there is no reason to suppose that victory will be secured by the particular minority to which one happens to belong. There are many minorities besides Communists: religious minorities, teetotal minorities, militarist minorities, capitalist minorities. Any one of these could adopt the method of obtaining power advocated by the Bolsheviks, and any one would be just as likely to succeed as they are. (PTB 146-7)

RIVALRY

Rivalry is, with most well-to-do energetic people, a stronger motive than love of money. Successful rivalry requires organization of rival forces; the tendency is for a business such as oil, for example, to organize itself into two rival groups, between them covering the world. They might, of course, combine, and they would no doubt increase their wealth if they did so. But combination would take the zest out of life. (I 34-5)

ROMAN PHILOSOPHY

Latin philosophers took over Greek theories. To the end, Rome was culturally parasitic on Greece. The Romans invented no art forms, constructed no original system of philosophy, and made no scientific discoveries. They made good roads, systematic legal codes, and efficient armies; for the rest they looked to Greece. (HWP 278)

ROMANS

The Romans discovered how to carry on the government of a great empire by means of a civil service and a body of law. (IPI 186)

ROMANTICISM

The Romantic Movement was essentially a protest in the name of the emotions against the previous undue emphasis upon the will. The Romantic Movement achieved something as regards the treatment of very young children, but in the main the educational authorities were too firmly entrenched and too much habituated to command to be appreciably affected by the softer ideals of the Romantics. (ESO 30)

The romantic movement is characterized, as a whole, by the substitution of aesthetic, for utilitarian standards. The earth-worm is useful, but not beautiful; the tiger is beautiful, but not useful. Darwin (who was not a romantic) praised the earth-worm; Blake praised the tiger. The morals of the romantics have primarily aesthetic motives. But in order to characterize the romantics, it is necessary to take account, not only of the importance of aesthetic motives, but also of the change of taste which made their sense of beauty different from that of their predecessors. (HWP 678)

ROUSSEAU

Rousseau appealed to the already existing cult of sensibility, and gave it a breadth and scope that it might not otherwise have possessed. He was a democrat, not only in his theories, but in his tastes. For long periods of his life, he was a poor vagabond, receiving kindness from people only slightly less destitute than himself. He repaid this kindness, in action, often with the blackest ingratitude, but in emotion his response was all that the most ardent devotee of sensibility could have wished. Having the tastes of a tramp, he found the restraints of Parisian society irksome. From him the romantics learned a contempt for the trammels of convention—first in dress and manners, in the minuet and the heroic couplet, then in art and love, and at last over the whole sphere of traditional morals. (HWP 676)

ROUTINE

Another respect in which, to my mind, many apostles of freedom go astray, is that they fail to recognize sufficiently the importance of routine in the life of the young. I do not mean that a routine should be rigid and absolute: there should be days when it is varied, such as Christmas Day and holidays. But even these variations should, on the whole, be expected by the child. A life of uncertainty is nervously exhausting at all times, but especially in youth. The child derives a sense of security from knowing more or less what is going to happen day by day. (ESO 37)

S

SABELLIANISM

The view which finally prevailed was that the Father and Son were equal, and of the same substance; they were, however, distinct Persons. The view that they were not distinct, but only different aspects of one Being, was the Sabellian heresy, called after its founder Sabellius. (HWP 333)

SABOTAGE

Sabotage is the practice of doing bad work, or spoiling machinery or work which has already been done, as a method of dealing with employers in a dispute when a strike appears for some reason undesirable or impossible. (RF 66)

SANCTIONS, MORAL

It is through the operation of praise and blame that the positive morality of a community becomes socially effective. (LAM 107)

SCAPEGOATS

The most curious form of this kind of transferred hatred is the habit of looking for scapegoats. In this case it is ourselves that we hate, but as this emotion is uncomfortable, we manage to heap all our own feelings of guilt upon some unfortunate victim. In the Old Testament the victim is a goat. This represents a humanitarian-reform, because at an earlier time the victim had been human. (TFD 42)

SCEPTICISM

The scepticism that I advocate amounts only to this: (1) that when the experts are agreed, the opposite opinion cannot be held to be certain; (2) that when they are not agreed, no opinion can be regarded as certain by a non-expert; and (3) that when they all hold that no sufficient grounds for a positive opinion exist, the ordinary man would do well to suspend his judgment. (SE 12-3)

Scepticism, while logically impeccable, is psychologically impossible, and there is an element of frivolous insincerity in any philosophy which pretends to accept it. Moreover, if scepticism is to be theoretically defensible, it must reject *all* inferences from what is experienced; a partial scepticism, such as the denial of physical events experienced by no one, or a solipsism which allows events in my future or in my unremembered past, has no logical justification since it must admit principles of inference which lead to beliefs that it rejects. (HK xi)

SCHOLASTICISM

Scholasticism, in its narrower sense, begins early in the twelfth century. As a philosophical school, it has certain definite characteristics. First, it is confined within the limits of what appears to the writer to be orthodoxy; if his views are condemned by a council, he is usually willing to retract. This is not to be attributed entirely to cowardice; it is analogous to the submission of a judge to the decision of a Court of Appeal. Second, within the limits of orthodoxy, Aristotle, who gradually became more fully known during the twelfth and thirteenth centuries, is increasingly accepted as the supreme authority; Plato no longer holds the first place. Third, there is a great belief in "dialectic" and in syllogistic reasoning; the general temper of the scholastics is minute and disputatious rather than mystical. Fourth, the question of universals is brought to the fore by the discovery that Aristotle and Plato do not agree about it; it would be a mistake to suppose, however, that universals are the main concern of the philosophers of this period. (HWP 435)

SCHOPENHAUER

His appeal has always been less to professional philosophers, than to artistic and literary people in search of a philosophy that they could believe. He began the emphasis upon Will which is characteristic of much nineteenth and twentieth-century philosophy; but for him Will, though metaphysically fundamental, is ethically evil—an opposition only possible for a pessimist. He acknowledged three sources of his philosophy, Kant, Plato, and the Upanishads, but I do not think he owes as much to Plato as he thinks he does. His outlook has a certain temperamental affinity with that of the Hellenistic age; it is tired and valetudinarian, valuing peace more than victory, and quietism more than attempts at reform, which he regards as inevitably futile. (HWP 753)

SECURITY, SENSE OF

I do not deny that something will be lost in the process of unification, but more will be preserved, and something of great value—namely a sense of security—will be gained. It is to such a consummation that our imagination and our long range political thinking must be directed. (KF 55)

SELF-FORGETFULNESS

I have spoken of men who were eminent in one way or another. But in actual fact I have been quite as often impressed by men and women of no eminence. What I have found most unforgettable is a certain kind of moral quality, a quality of self-forgetfulness, whether in private life, in public affairs, or in the pursuit of truth. (UE 171)

SELLING, PSYCHOLOGY OF

The ultimate psychological source of our preference for selling over buying is that we prefer power to pleasure. This is not a universal characteristic; there are spendthrifts, who like a short life and a merry one. But it is a characteristic of the energetic, successful individuals who give the tone to a competitive age. (IPI 86)

SENSATION

We shall give the name "sensation" to the experience of being immediately aware of these things. Thus, whenever we see a colour, we have a sensation *of* the colour, but the colour itself is a sense-datum, not a sensation. (PP 17)

And finally it is by no means certain that the peculiar causal laws which govern mental events are not really physiological. The law of habit, which is one of the most distinctive, may be fully explicable in terms of the peculiarities of nervous tissue, and these peculiarities, in turn, may be explicable by the laws of physics. It seems, therefore, that we are driven to a different kind of definition. It is for this reason that it was necessary to develop the definition of perception. With this definition, we can define a sensation as the non-mnemic elements in a perception. (AM 139)

SENSE-DATA

If we have been right in our contentions, sense-data are merely those among the ultimate constituents of the physical world of which we happen to be immediately aware; they themselves are purely physical, and all that is mental in connection with them is our awareness of them, which is irrelevant to their nature and to their place in physics. (ML 143)

SENSIBILIA

I shall give the name *sensibilia* to those objects which have the same metaphysical and physical status as sense-data, without necessarily being data to any mind. Thus the relation of a *sensibile* to a sense-datum is like that of a man to a husband: a man becomes a husband by entering into the relation of marriage, and similarly a *sensibile* becomes a sense-datum by entering into the relation of acquaintance. (ML 148-9)

SENSITIVENESS

A purely theoretical definition would be that a person is emotionally sensitive when many stimuli produce emotions in him; but taken thus broadly the quality is not necessarily a good one. If sensitiveness is to be good, the emotional reaction must be in some sense *appropriate:* mere intensity is not what is needed. The quality I have in mind is that of being affected pleasurably or the reverse by many things, and by the right things. (EEC 69-70)

SENTENCES

Thus the correct use of relational words, i.e. of sentences, involves what may be correctly termed "perception of form", i.e. it involves a definite reaction to a stimulus which is a form. Suppose, for example, that a child has learnt to say that one thing is "above" another when this is in fact the case. The stimulus to the use of the word "above" is a relational feature of the environment, and we may say that this feature is "perceived" since it produces a definite reaction. It may be said that the relation *above* is not very like the word "above." That is true; but the same is true of ordinary physical objects. A stone, according to the physicists, is not at all like what we see when we look at it, and yet we may be correctly said to "perceive" it. This, however, is to anticipate. The definite point which has emerged is that, when a person can use sentences correctly, that is a proof of sensitiveness to formal or relational stimuli. (OP 56)

We must now define "sentence" and "having the same meaning." Ignoring the latter for the moment, what is a sentence? It may be a single word, or, more usually, a number of words put together according to the laws of syntax; but what distinguishes it is that it expresses something of the nature of an assertion, a denial, an imperative, a desire, or a question. What is more remarkable about a sentence, from our point of view, is that we can understand what it expresses if we know the meaning of its several words and the rules of syntax. (IMT 10-1)

SENTENCES, MOLECULAR

Sentences containing conjunctions I shall call "molecular" sentences, the "p" and "q" which are conjoined being conceived as the "atoms." Given the truth or falsehood of a set of propositions, the truth or falsehood of every molecular proposition constructed out of the set follows by syntactical rules, and requires no fresh observation of facts. We are, in fact, in the domain of logic. (HK 120)

SEX

The whole conception of sex as a matter of natural delight, rising on occasion to poetry, sometimes lighthearted and gay, sometimes passionate with a tragic profundity, lies outside the purview of the pedagogic moralists, to whom sex is wicked when it is combined with delight, and virtuous only when it is drab and habitual. Poetry and joy and beauty are thrust out of life by this morality of ugliness, and something stark and rigid is brought into all human relationships. From this outlook come prudery and pettymindedness and the death of imagination. It may be that a freer outlook also has its dangers. But they are the dangers of life, not of death. (ESO 124-5)

SEX EDUCATION

Answering questions is a major part of sex education. Two rules cover the ground. First, always give a truthful answer to a question; secondly, regard sex knowledge as exactly like any other knowledge. (EEC 213)

SEXUAL INTERCOURSE

Men desire sexual intercourse, but they do not as a rule desire children strongly or often. Yet without the hope of children and its occasional realization, sexual intercourse remains for most people an isolated and separate pleasure, not uniting their personal life with the life of mankind, not continuous with the central purposes by which they live, and not capable of bringing that profound sense of fulfilment which comes from completion by children. (PSR 231)

SEXUAL MORALITY

Sexual morality, freed from superstition, is a simple matter. Fraud and deceit, assault, seduction of persons under age, are proper matters for the criminal law. Relations between adults who are free agents are a private matter, and should not be interfered with either by the law or by public opinion, because no outsider can know whether they are good or bad. When children are involved the state becomes interested to the extent of seeing that they are properly educated and cared for, and it ought to insure that the father does his duty by them in the way of maintenance. But neither the state nor public opinion ought to insist on the parents living together if they are incompatible; the spectacle of parents' quarrels is far worse for children than the separation of the parents could possibly be. (SIE 14)

SHREWDNESS

Shrewdness when it is genuine, belongs more to the unconscious than to the conscious part of our nature. It is, I suppose, the main quality required for success in business. From a moral point of view, it is a humble quality, since it is always selfish; yet it suffices to keep men from the worst crimes. (SE 21)

SIN

The conception of sin which is bound up with Christian ethics is one that does an extraordinary amount of harm, since it affords people an outlet for their sadism which they believe to be legitimate and even noble. (RUC 8)

SLAVE LABOR CAMPS

In Russia the inhumanities not unlike those of the Congo and of early British industrialism are inflicted in the forced labor camps which have become an integral part of the Soviet economy. Human nature is not to be trusted with irresponsible power, and where irresponsible power exists, appalling cruelties are to be expected. (BOD 16)

SOCIAL COHESION
Social cohesion, which started with loyalty to a group reinforced by the fear of enemies, grew by processes partly natural and partly deliberate until it reached the vast conglomerations that we now know as nations. (AAI 16)

SOCIALISM
Let us begin by a definition of Socialism. The definition must consist of two parts, economic and political. The economic part consists in State ownership of ultimate economic power, which involves, as a minimum, land and minerals, capital, banking, credit and foreign trade. The political part requires that the ultimate political power should be democratic. (IPI 140-1)

SOLITUDE
A certain degree of isolation both in space and time is essential to generate the independence required for the most important work; there must be something which is felt to be of more importance than the admiration of the contemporary crowd. We are suffering not from the decay of theological beliefs but from the loss of solitude. (UE 69-70)

SOPHISTS
This explains the popularity of the Sophists with one class and their unpopularity with another. But in their own minds they served more impersonal purposes, and it is clear that many of them were genuinely concerned with philosophy. Plato devoted himself to caricaturing and vilifying them, but they must not be judged by his polemics. (HWP 75)

SOUL, THE
The "soul," as it first appeared in Greek thought, had a religious though not a Christian origin. It seems, so far as

Greece was concerned, to have originated in the teaching of the Pythagoreans, who believed in transmigration, and aimed at an ultimate salvation which was to consist of liberation from the bondage to matter which the soul must suffer so long as it is attached to a body. The Pythagoreans influenced Plato, and Plato influenced the Fathers of the Church; in this way the doctrine of the soul as something distinct from the body became part of Christian doctrine. Other influences entered in, notably that of Aristotle and that of the Stoics; but Platonism, particularly in its later forms, was the most important pagan element in patristic philosophy. (RAS 114-5)

W

WAR
The argument from history is very apt to be fallacious as applied to modern conditions. War is a more serious matter than it used to be. War can still settle problems, but it can only settle them the wrong way. (MRW 174)

WAR, CAUSES OF
There are two opposite forces that tend to produce great wars. On the one hand, there is the overweening ambition of the strong; on the other hand, there is the discontent of the less fortunate nations. (PPW 93)

WAR, CHANGES IN TECHNIQUE OF
Changes in the technique of war have had more influence upon the course of history than is supposed by those whose attention is mainly centred upon economic causation. There has been, since the beginning of organized fighting, an oscillation between superiority of the defensive and superiority of the offensive. Broadly speaking, when the defensive is strong civilization makes progress,

and when the offensive is strong men revert towards barbarism. (WWP 16)

WAR, COMING OF

War comes only when the opposing forces are roughly equal, for if there is an obvious preponderance on either side the other side gives way. (CAN 8)

WAR, FEAR OF

If a world government is ever to succeed, fear will still be the cement holding it together, but it will be a new kind of fear—a fear of anarchy and destruction and annihilation of whole populations, not the fear of this or that group of dastardly foreigners. (KF 54)

WAR OF PRESTIGE

The last kind of war we have to consider is what I have called "the war of prestige." Prestige is seldom more than one element in the causes of a war, but it is often a very important element. (JWT 36)

WAR OF PRINCIPLE

The second type of war which may sometimes be justified is what may be called "the war of principle." To this kind belong the wars of Protestant and Catholic, and the English and American civil wars. In such cases, each side, or at least one side, is honestly convinced that the progress of mankind depends upon the adoption of certain beliefs or institutions, which through blindness or natural depravity, the other side will not regard as reasonable, except when presented at the point of the bayonet. (JWT 31)

Force used in defence of the law, when it is sufficiently serious, comes under the head of "wars of principle". A contest between one burglar and the whole police force can hardly be dignified with the name of war, but the suppression of an insurrection which has no general impersonal objects is essentially analogous to the suppression of an individual criminal, and may involve very serious acts of war. If an international government is ever formed, it will be very important to establish its authority, and wars waged by it against recalcitrant States will be in defence of the law. (WWP 114-5)

WAR OF SELF-DEFENCE

The next kind of war to be considered is the war of self-defence. This kind of war is almost universally admitted to be justifiable, and is condemned only by Christ and Tolstoy. The justification of wars of self-defence is very convenient, since so far as I know there has never yet been a war which was not one of self-defence. (JWT 34)

WAVE-NUMBER

In studying the connection between the different lines in the spectrum of an element, it is convenient to characterize a wave, not by its wave-length, but by its "wave-number," which means the number of waves in a centimetre. Thus if the wave-length is one ten-thousandth of a centimetre, the wave-number is 10,000; if the wave-length is one hundred-thousandth of a centimetre, the wave-number is 100,000, and so on. (ABCA 43)

WILL

It remains to say a few words about "will." There is a sense in which will is an observable phenomenon, and another in which it is a metaphysical superstition. It is obvious that I can say, "I will hold my breath for thirty seconds," and proceed to do so; that I can say, "I will go to America," and proceed to do so; and so on. In this sense, will is an observable phenomenon. But as a faculty, as a separate occur-rence, it is, I think, a delusion. (OP 223)

WILL, HUMAN

There is no external compulsion for a man to act other-wise than as he wishes except in the obvious ways that common sense recognizes. No man can resist torture be-yond a point, and a scientific tyrant can always secure obe-dience if his victim has not the means of suicide. A man may also be constrained by insanity to commit acts for which the law does not hold him responsible. But it is mere mythology to imagine a semipersonal pagan god or god-dess regulating the lives of men or of nations in a manner independent of human will. (TRF 5)

WILL, THE GENERAL

I come now to the doctrine of the general will, which is both important and obscure. The general will is not identi-cal with the will of the majority, or even with the will of all the citizens. It seems to be conceived as the will belonging to the body politic as such. If we take Hobbes's view, that a civil society is a person, we must suppose it is endowed with the attributes of personality, including will. But then we are faced with the difficulty of deciding what are the vis-ible manifestations of this will, and here Rousseau leaves us in the dark. We are told that the general will is always right and always tends to the public advantage; but that it does not follow that the deliberations of the people are equally correct, for there is often a great deal of difference between the will of all and the general will. How, then, are we to know what is the general will? (HWP 697-8)

WILL-TO-DOUBT

William James used to preach the "will-to-believe." For my part, I should wish to preach the "will-to-doubt." None of our beliefs is quite true; all have at least a penumbra of vagueness and error. (FT 14)

KEY TO SYMBOLS

AA	Americans Are ... The Impact of America upon European Culture (1950)
AAI	Authority and the Individual (1949)
ABCA	The ABC of Atoms (1923)
ABCR	The ABC of Relativity (1925)
AM	The Analysis of Mind (1921)
AOM	The Analysis of Mutter (1927)
APFY	A Philosophy for You in These Times (1941)
API	The Amberley Papers, Volume I. (1937)
AWF	A World Federation (1941)
BOD	Boredom or Doom in a Scientific World (1948)
BW	Bolshevism and the West (1924)
CAB	Can America and Britain be Friends? (1944)
CAN	If War Comes Can America Stay Neutral? (1939)
CAW	Carroll's Alice in Wonderland (1942)
CGS	Citizenship in a Great State (1943)
CH	The Conquest of Happiness (1930)
CTR	Came the Revolution ... (1950)
CWA	Can We Afford to Keep Open Minds? (1950)
DAE	Democracy and Economics (1939)
DDM	Descartes' Discourse on Method (1942)

DMC	Divorce by Mutual Consent (1930)
DNL	Dewey's New Logic (1939)
EAW	Education after the War (1943)
EDTF	On the Evils Due to Fear (1929)
EEC	On Education Especially in Early Childhood (1926)
EIU	Education in International Understanding (1944)
ER	The Essence of Religion (1912)
ESO	Education and the Social Order (1932)
FAC	Freedom and the Colleges (1940)
FAG	Freedom and Government (1940)
FAH	How to be Free and Happy (1924)
FAR	The Faith of a Rationalist (1947)
FIE	Freedom in Education (1923)
FO	Freedom and Organization (1934)
FOD	The Future of Democracy (1937)
FOP	Future of Pacifism (1944)
FT	Free Thought and Official Propaganda (1922)
GAT	A Guide for Living in the Atomic Age (1949)
GBP	Government by Propaganda (1924)
HCS	The High Cost of Survival (1949)
HFA	Hopes and Fears as Regards America (1922)
HK	Human Knowledge: Its Scope and Limits (1948)
HPH	Hegel's Philosophy of History (1941)
HWP	A History of Western Philosophy (1945)
I	Icarus, or the Future of Science (1924)
IMP	Introduction to Mathematical Philosophy (1919)
IMT	An Inquiry into Meaning and Truth (1940)
ING	Introduction to The New Generation (1930)
IPI	In Praise of Idleness (1935)
ISI	Is Security Increasing? (1939)
ISIP	The International Significance of the Indian Problem (1943)

PSR	Principles of Social Reconstruction (1916)
PTB	The Practice and Theory of Bolshevism (1920)
RAS	Religion and Science (1935)
RF	Roads to Freedom (1917)
RTC	Reply to Criticisms (1944)
RUC	Has Religion Made Useful Contributions to Civilization? (1930)
S	Science (1928)
SAE	Science and Education (1928)
SC	Social Cohesion and Human Nature (1948)
SE	Sceptical Essays (1928)
SIE	Styles in Ethics (1924)
SO	The Scientific Outlook (1931)
SPE	Spinoza's Ethics (1942)
SSl	Science and Social Institutions (1938)
STGS	Still Time for Good Sense (1947)
STS	The Science to Save Us from Science (1950)
TEP	Taming Economic Power (1938)
TFD	To Face Danger without Hysteria (1951)
TRF	To Replace Our Fears with Hope (1950)
TWI	Is a Third War Inevitable? (1950)
TWW	Three Ways to the World (1922)
UE	Unpopular Essays (1951)
WIB	What I Believe (1925)
WIBII	What I Believe (1929)
WIG	Where is Industrialism Going? (1923)
WIH	What is Happiness? (1939)
WMD	When Should Marriage be Dissolved? (1912)
WNC	Why I am Not a Christian (1927)
WNCO	Why I am Not a Communist (1934)
WRU	Why Radicals are Unpopular (1936)
WWP	Which Way to Peace? (1936)
ZPS	Zionism and the Peace Settlement (1943)

ACKNOWLEDGEMENTS

Acknowledgements are due primarily to Lord Russell for his kind permission to make the extensive selections from his works represented here. The choices were that of the editor and the fault resultant from the annoying, though necessary, foreshortening of exposition and argument is entirely his; so, too, are the errors of omission, though space was a contributing factor. The editor is deeply grateful for the generous consent and the interest expressed by Lord Russell as this volume grew.

Our thanks are also due to Lord Russell's publishers:

George Allen & Unwin, Ltd.: A Critical Exposition of the Philosophy of Leibniz; Our Knowledge of the External World, Principles of Social Reconstruction, Justice in War-Time, Roads to Freedom, Introduction to Mathematical Philosophy, Practice and Theory of Bolshevism, The Analysis of Mind, The Problem of China, Free Thought and Official Propaganda, Prospects of Industrial Civilization, Logical Atomism, Science and Social Institutions, Science and Education, Mysticism and Logic, In Praise of Idleness, An Outline of Philosophy, On Education Especially in Early Childhood, The Conquest of Happiness, Education and the Social Order, Sceptical Essays, Inquiry into Meaning and

Truth, The Scientific Outlook, Power, Human Knowledge, Marriage and Morals, Authority and the Individual, Freedom versus Organization, History of Western Philosophy, Unpopular Essays, Bolshevism and the West, Bolshevism in Theory and Practice.

The American Mercury: Our Sexual Ethics, Freedom and the College, Education after the War.

The American Scholar: The Future of Pacifism.

Appleton-Century-Crofts, Inc.: Letter in "The World's Best." Political Ideals, Prospects of Industrial Civilization.

Arco Publishing Company: Some Problems of the Post War World, The International Significance of the Indian Problem.

The Beacon Press: The Political and Cultural Influence; Last Chance.

The Century Magazine: Where is Industrialism Going?, If We are to Prevent the Next War.

The University of Chicago Round Table: Taming Economic Power, Is Security Increasing?

The Citadel Press: Introduction to "The New Generation."

Columbia University Press: The Impact of Science on Society.

Common Sense: Why Radicals are Unpopular, If War Comes—Can America Stay Neutral?

The John Day Company: Divorce by Mutual Consent.

The Dial Magazine: Leisure and Mechanism, Freedom in Education: A Protest against Mechanism, Life in the Middle Ages.

E. P. Dutton & Co.: The ABC of Atoms, Icarus or the Future of Science, What I Believe.

The Encyclopedia Britannica Company, Ltd.: Government by propaganda.

The English Review: When Should Marriage be Dissolved?

Fortune Magazine: Citizenship in a Great State.

Magazine '47: Still Time For Good Sense.

Haldeman-Julius Company: An Outline of Intellectual Rubbish, Ideas that Have Harmed Mankind, Ideas that Have Helped Mankind.

Harcourt, Brace & Co.: Bolshevism: Practice and Theory, Freedom and Government, The Analysis of Matter.

Harper & Brothers: ABC of Relativity, On the Evils Due to Fear, Foreword to Feibleman's An Introduction to Pierce's Philosophy, Democracy and Education.

Harper's Magazine: The Functions of a Teacher.

The New York Herald Tribune (This Week): The High Cost of Survival.

The Hibbert Journal: The Essence of Religion.

Hogarth Press: The Amberley Papers.

Independent Review: On History.

International Journal of Ethics: Marriage and the Population Question.

Michael Joseph, Ltd.: Which Way to Peace?

The New Leader: A World Federation.

Library of Living Philosophers, Inc.: My Mental Development, Reply to Criticisms, Dewey's New Logic, The Philosophy of Santayana.

The Listener (The British Broadcasting Corporation): Social Cohesion and Human Nature.

Liveright Publishing Corporation: Why Men Fight, Styles in Ethics, Education and the Good Life, The Conquest of Happiness, Marriage and Morals.

Longmans, Green & Co.: Science.

The Macmillan Company: Introduction to Mathematical Philosophy, The Analysis of Mind, Logical Atomism, Science and Social Institutions.

The Modern Library (Random House, Inc.): Introduction to

Selected Papers of Bertrand Russell, Hegel's Philosophy of History, Descartes' Discourse on Method, Spinoza's Ethics, Carroll's Alice in Wonderland.

Modern Monthly: Why I am not a Communist.

The Nation: Munich Rather than War. Must Democracy Use Force?, The Superior Virtue of the Oppressed.

National Book League: Philosophy and Politics

The New Palestine: Zionism and the Peace Settlement.

The New Republic: Hopes and Fears as Regards America; The Future of Democracy.

The New York Times: Letter on the Bertrand Russell Case.

The New York Times Magazine: The Science to Save Us from Science, Can We Afford to Keep Open Minds?, If We are to Survive This Dark Time, The Kind of Fear We Sorely Need, To Replace Our Hopes with Fears, To Face Danger without Hysteria.

W. W. Norton & Company, Inc.: Our Knowledge of the External World, Mysticism and Logic, Philosophy, In Praise of Idleness, Education and the Modern World, Sceptical Essays, Inquiry into Meaning and Truth, The Scientific Outlook, Power, The Amberley Papers, Freedom versus Organization.

Open Court Publishing Company: Justice in War-Time.

Oxford University Press: Religion and Science, Problems of Philosophy.

C. P. Putnam's Sons: What is Happiness?

Rand School of Social Science: How to be Free and Happy.

Rationalist Press Association: The Faith of a Rationalist, Why I am not a Christian.

The Reader's Digest: A Philosophy for You in These Times.

Routledge and Kegan Paul, Ltd.: ABC of Atoms, Icarus, ABC of Relativity, What I Believe, Analysis of Matter.

St. Louis Post Dispatch: Science and Education.

Saturday Evening Post: Can Americans and British be Friends?

Saturday Review of Literature: Came the Revolution.

Simon & Schuster, Inc.: What I Believe, Living Philosophy Revised.